PROMOTION:

How can someone be center-brained?

Notice that when one would say, "Oh, there's a right hemisphere and there's a left hemisphere," that's only two. Is it possible for there to be a third dimension to the hemispheres of the brain? Can there actually be a third area - a brain center or center-brain - that helps to control our thinking and our actions? I believe so ... The concept of "center-brained" would presumably imply a balance or integration of both left-brained and right-brained characteristics, causing a person to effectively utilize both logical and creative thinking processes ...

Can it be that when one is trending towards the dominant use of one side, and something occurs to interrupt that process, we don't really become right or left brain-dominant but hover somewhere in the middle? And if this is so, can the fact that we are neither left-hand nor right-hand dominant, also correlate with our inability to differentiate left from right?... Also, is it far-fetched to think that while the right hemisphere will dominate in some functions, and the left hemisphere will dominate in some functions, that the middle section, perhaps encompassing a part of the right and left hemispheres, and, the corpus callosum, can also dominate in some functions? If this is indeed the case, that accounts for the fact that when I ask my brain which hand is my dominant hand, it cannot respond. As a center-brained person, I have no dominant side!

CENTER
BRAINED

CENTER BRAINED

**WHY YOU CAN'T TELL LEFT FROM RIGHT,
EAST FROM WEST, OR NORTH FROM SOUTH**

E. Patsy Greenland

JACINTH MEDIA
PRODUCTIONS

Published by Jacinth Media Productions

Jacinth Media Productions® is a registered trademark.

Printed in the United States of America.

Library of Congress Control Number: 2025907339

ISBN:
987-1-960594-31-0 - Hardback
978-1-960594-32-7 - Paperback
978-1-960594-33-4 - ePUB

This publication is designed to provide accurate and authoritative information with regard to the subject matter covered. It is sold with the understanding that the publisher is not engaged in rendering legal, accounting, or other professional advice. If legal advice or other expert assistance is required, the services of a competent professional should be sought. The opinions expressed by the author in this book are not endorsed by Jacinth Media Productions® and are the sole responsibility of the author rendering the opinion.

For more information, please write:
Jacinth Media Productions
607 N 9th Street, Allentown PA 18102;
Email: info@jacinthmediaproductions.com

Disclaimer

For the most part, the opinions expressed in this book are my own, born out of sixty plus years of studying my own experiences as a directionally challenged person. I stand by everything I've said about myself. I also endorse the comments of others who are also directionally challenged, for the simple reason that I have also had those experiences. There is however, also a significant dependence on the work of several neurologists and other scientists. I present their findings as expert information which I am not in a position to verify. I therefore highly recommend that readers of this book do their own research and consult the appropriate health service provider, on the matters relating to their health and particularly with respect to any symptoms that may require a medical or psychological diagnosis or treatment.

Dedicated to:

*All who have ever been criticized
for losing their way*

Acknowledgements

"For God hath not given us the spirit of fear; but of power, and of love, and of a sound mind."
II Tim 1:7.

I thank Him for carrying me through many lost and lonesome valleys.

I also thank the many navigationally oriented persons who have sympathized with, and helped me along the way, and I'll be eternally grateful to all those who are like me, and who commiserated with me and shared their stories with me.

Special thanks go to the Face Book group: Directional Disorientation (aka Developmental Topographical Disorientation), in particular, to those who permitted me to chronicle their comments, to Dr. Benton St Cyr for his insightful suggestions; to my daughter, Kerrolyn, my son Kerrol, and my husband, Victor, for all that you did, are doing now, and will continue to do for me.

Contents

Preface

I dare say that if you are not directionally challenged, you certainly know at least one person who is. Surely, if it's not you, you must be acquainted with someone who struggles to differentiate between left and right or who finds it challenging to distinguish east, west, north, and south. But have you ever pondered how many people in the world are directionally challenged? And have you ever contemplated why some individuals find it so difficult to navigate and orient themselves?

Being lost is not fun. It brings serious suffering, not just on the lost, but on those who must search for, and sometimes, never find, the lost. There is a group of individuals who get lost very often, and although some of them may eventually find their way, or they may eventually be found, their suffering is not less painful. They suffer in silence, and when they get lost, they constantly worry that their current situation could be repeated several times in a day, for as many more days, weeks, months and years, as they will live.

These are concerns about which I have pondered through-out my entire life, always with a view that, at some point in time, I would shine a light on them. Well, that time has come. I am now ready to reveal to the rest of the world, the vicissitudes of the daily lives of the directionally challenged. I do not intend to stop at merely exposing the trials directionally challenged people face each day, but I also want to highlight solutions to our present predicament.

I'm writing for those people, whose stories have never been told, who feel real terror every time they must move from one location to another, whether or not they have taken such a trip before. I'm writing for directionally challenged individuals, who, like me, are misunderstood and mischaracterized by those who have never walked a mile in our shoes.

I must say, up front, that I am not a medical expert. But I'm someone who has lived and studied the life of a directionally challenged person; and who has been ultra-sensitive in detecting others who are directionally challenged, for well over sixty years. I have spent a great deal of time considering, researching, and defending people in this situation. This book does deal with some of the possible physiological and psychological reasons for directional disorientation, as the condition is sometimes called; but it mainly gives explanations and experiences from the layman's perspective.

I have also conversed with experts on the human mind. I have read scores of scholarly dissertations, and am gratified that many of the theories I espoused at the beginning of my quest, have been corroborated. For example, I maintained for years that I was neither left-brained nor right-brained; that I am, in fact center-brained. I can now say that based on what I have learned; my theory is correct. I have learned so much more, however, and can now truly say that I know why I am directionally challenged.

This book is largely about how I have fared as a directionally challenged person, because I know myself best. But it is also about the scores of persons whose experiences have informed me, challenged me, and encouraged me. It explains the concept of *directional challenge* or *confusion*, which has several other terms of reference. Many of these can be found in the Glossary, along with definitions of other technical terms mentioned. It explores the notion of how our brain controls all aspects of our cognition and navigation; of our orientation and locomotion. It highlights the fact that one's navigational orientation can be determined by one side of our brain or the other side, as well as a collaboration of both sides. It demonstrates that the functions of one side of the brain can be assumed by the other, and that one side of the brain evidently controls functioning on the opposite side of the body, hence a right-brain-dominant person will be functionally left-handed. The book seeks to determine how much of our navigational confusion is caused by a difference in the way our brains innately function, or if our navigational confusion is due to adverse circumstances, to inappropriately phrased and placed directions; to instructions and devices created solely by and for one particular group, or if it's due to our reluctance to push past our inabilities. I've also tried to give practical suggestions on how directional confusion can be recognized, reduced and/or eliminated.

My aim is also to highlight what has already been discovered about directional challenge or confusion. I hope that as you follow my meanderings, you too, will get a better understanding of what it means to be directionally challenged, and that together, we will endeavor to point the way forward.

E. Patsy G

Foreword

I have known E Patsy Greenland for the past seven (7) years, but it seems that we've been together all our lives. We share the same faith and are kindred spirits in many ways. We worked very closely on my first publication and I benefited greatly from her kind, contributions. From the use of her computer, when mine was out of order, to editing and proof reading my work, as well as encouraging me to press on, when I met with obstacles, I have always had her unswerving support.

E. Patsy has already published her first book, *"Thoughts and Tales that Inspire."* It was as I attended the launch of this book that I resolved to embark on own my publishing path, and E Patsy has not only shared her practical experience with me, but since my book was about Jesus Christ, as a committed and sincere Christian, with a wealth of knowledge borne out of being a Seventh-day Adventist, she was able to point out little nuances that would have detracted from the truth as it is in Jesus.

I knew that E. Patsy had an aversion to driving and venturing into strange regions, but I didn't know about her directional challenge until she explained it. In fact, I did not think that the inability to navigate and to identify left and right was such a widespread issue until she highlighted it. Now I'm glad she did. I hope that all who read this book will come to recognize, acknowledge, and/or understand the challenges faced by people who are unable to orient themselves, and to navigate. Once not just the problem, but some of the causes are identified, I know that E. Patsy will be leading the charge towards forming a global coalition to devise strategies for alleviating and or eliminating the issues caused by this situation.

P. Dalton Simms
August 20, 2024

Author of: *A boy named Jesus*
The Gamblers: The tested & tried life of a pastor
Who really are the Rainbow People?
Is Jehovah universally the only Supreme God?

1
No, we're not stupid!

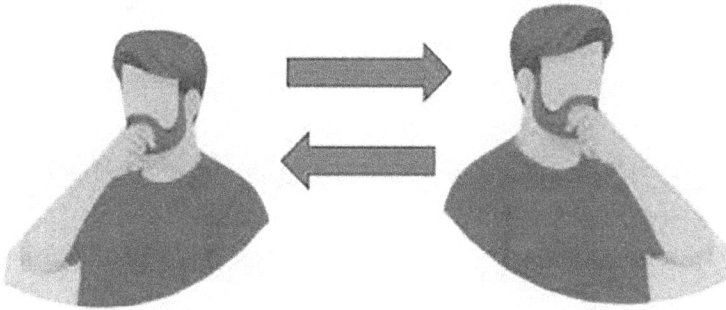

Do you find yourself utterly perplexed whenever someone points out something as being on your right or left?

Despite having a theoretical understanding that if you're facing north, south is behind you, west is to your left, and east is to your right, do you still struggle to apply this knowledge in real-world situations? Similarly, do you know that if you're facing east, west is behind you, north is to your left, and south is to your right? If you do, why does this understanding seem to elude you when it comes to practical application? Why is it such a challenge to translate basic directional knowledge into everyday activities?

When you visit your doctor's office, do you need help getting to the exit, after barging into several offices and storerooms in your quest to get out? Or, at the supermarket, have you ever got to the check-out and found that "your trolley" has items you did not put there, because, somewhere along those aisles, you "lost" your trolley, and just grabbed one that you thought was yours? If that has happened to you, you're probably like me. It happens to me all the time. I usually park my trolley at the end of an aisle, walk along the aisles and pick up my items, then return to the trolley with an armful of bottles, bags and packages. But, with my propensity for lostness, I'll invariably dump them in the wrong place, and move off with someone else's trolley. As a friend and I laughed over this shared tendency, we wondered why no one has ever called us out about it.

Even more unsettling, have you ever been driving home, only to be suddenly hit with sheer panic, as you discovered that you had no idea where you were, even though you were making a trip you have undertaken countless times?

If you've had any of those experiences, note that I have had all of them so often, that I now take them for granted. Consider this: I'm at a restaurant that my husband and I frequent. I leave our table to visit the ladies' room. At the end of my visit, it takes me twice as long to get back to the table, as it took to get to the restroom, because when I exit the restroom, I don't know which way to go!

Invariably, I go in the wrong direction. It's especially difficult, if we're doing night dining, and the lights in the restaurant are dimmed. Most times I make sure that I have my phone with me, and I have to call my husband, and ask him to either stand, or raise his hand!

The startling truth is that there are thousands and thousands; I believe millions, and perhaps billions of people the world over, who have had most if not all of those experiences.

THE BACK-STORY

Let me tell you a little about myself. The first phase of my academic life was spent in a one-room schoolhouse. At one corner of this room, there was the class for the six-year-olds. I was seven years old, at the time, and my class was to another side. One day, I was minding my own business, doing my work, but because it was a one room school, I could hear the activities going on in the other classes. This other class was, I can now say, to my left. But I didn't know that, then. It was just another class, over there. That day, the teacher was teaching Composition Writing. I remember it very clearly. I even remember her name. She was Mrs. Walcott. She stood in front of her class, and she said, "Make a sentence about me." As several of the children put their hands up, she pointed to one child, and the child said, "My teacher is standing in front of the class." Mrs. Walcott said, "Oh! Very good!" And she wrote that sentence on the board. Then she said, "Give me another sentence." Several hands went up again, and some children said things that perhaps she wasn't too happy with. But then one little girl put her hand up and the teacher said, "Okay, go ahead." The child said, "She has a box of chalk in her hand." Mrs. Walcott said, "Very observant. Very good." She wrote that sentence on the board, then she said to the class, "Tell me another sentence." Again, there were some suggestions, to which she said, "Oh, yes. Tell me another one." Finally, the same girl who had spoken about the box of chalk, put her hand up again. When the teacher acknowledged her, she said, "She has it in her left hand." The teacher said, "Wonderful!" And she wrote that sentence on the board.

After that, I stopped listening to them and was wondering to myself, "How on earth does this little child know that the teacher has the chalk box in her left hand?" I was older than her, and I had no idea how to identify left and right. I didn't have any idea then, and I don't have any idea now.

However, that particular incident has helped me tremendously, throughout my life, because whenever someone says anything about my left hand or my right hand, I recall the image of Mrs. Walcott, standing in front of her class. I visualize the hand that held that chalk box. I know that it was her left hand that held it - because the child said so - and I mentally superimpose myself on that image and then I can say, "Okay. Yeah. If I were Mrs. Walcott, standing in front of her class, this would be the hand holding the chalk box. Therefore, this is my left hand. And if this is my left hand, my other hand is my right hand." That's how I have gone through life, identifying left and right. The one drawback is that this analysis is time-consuming, so in an emergency, instead of doing it, I guess. Nine out of ten times, when I guess, I am wrong.

Also, Phonics was a subject used to teach us to read. The teacher said, m-a-n spelled the word man, and m-e-n spelled the word men. Later, she would say, "M-a-n-y spells the word many" (pronounced men-ee).

I could not accept that. As far as I could see and understand, based on what I had been taught, m-a-n-y was man-ee, not men-ee. So, when she wrote sentences on the board, and instructed us to copy the sentences to our books, if the sentences contained the word *many*, I had to make a little adjustment to what she wrote. I just thought that there was something not right about writing m-a-n-y as many - pronounced men-ee. So, every time this teacher wrote the word, *many* on the board. I would write it in my book as *meny*. She would call me to her table. She would explain to me that the official language (we were using back then in Jamaica), was the "Queen's English" and if the queen thought that m-a-n-y should be pronounced as men-ee, then who was I to want to change that? Now, I don't think that I was a rude or contrary child. But what she was saying just would not compute. And because it would not compute, I could not bring myself to write m-a-n-y as many (pronounced men-ee).

So, this teacher would punish me, every time I "misspelled" the word. To force her point home, she would make an effort to write a sentence with that word on the board every day. And every day, when I copied what she wrote I would change m-a-n-y to m-e-n-y, and she would punish me. This matter became the talk among the teachers, because my teacher told the others about this stubborn (she used another phrase) girl in her class who wanted to change the Queen's English. Like I said, I was not being rebellious or stubborn. I just could not accept what she said, because my brain is wired differently.

Eventually, I became tired of being punished, every day, and for being the subject of discussion among the teachers, every day. Even the other children in my class began teasing me, saying how stupid I was for inviting punishment, every day! So, after a while, I gave up writing the word meny. However, to this day, I still say that m-a-n-y should be pronounced as man-ee.

In the identical manner that I could not accept the pronunciation of "many," I could not, still cannot, grasp the explanation of left and right, of east, west, north and south.

Now don't get me wrong. I believe I'm intelligent, and I know you are too. I hold a Bachelor's degree in Communication and a Master's degree in Health Administration. I am sure that you are a top performer at your job, or at school, having achieved, or will soon be achieving even higher academic accolades. You are sociable, successful, very well accomplished in most aspects of life. Yet, when it comes to telling right from left, you're a complete disaster. Do you know of anyone else that is like you in this aspect? If you do not, don't worry. There are many people who are just like you. If you are directionally challenged, I am here to let you know that you are not stupid, and you're actually in good company. As I've said, there are many, many people, the world over who experience varying degrees of difficulty navigating their way through life. Many of these people may have been told that they are at various points on a spectrum of some syndrome. Others are even told that they have a birth defect, or, they may have sustained brain damage at some point, or that they are, quite plainly, stupid.

We're just directionally challenged!

"I visited my husband in the hospital for three weeks. Even at the end of his stay, I still couldn't work out which direction I should take when I stepped out of the lift." - Teresa H.

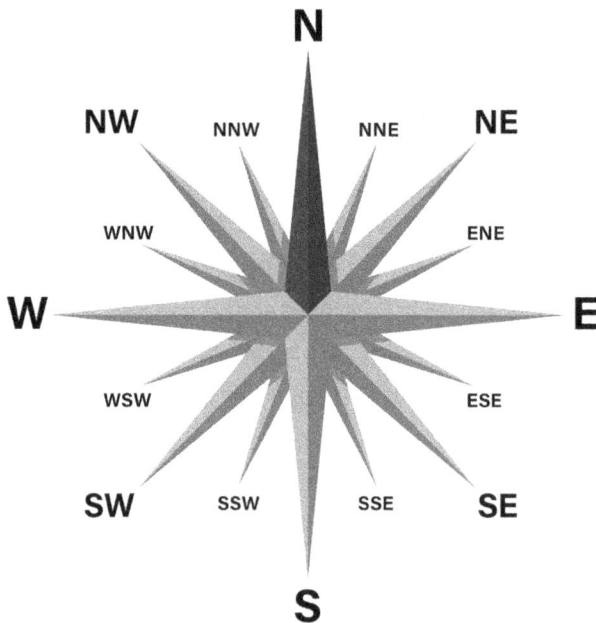

Have you ever found yourself lost on a familiar route, perhaps because you took a right turn instead of a left? Or maybe you went east when you should have gone west? Do you wonder why remembering directions seems so easy for others, but nigh impossible for you? If so, don't worry. You're not alone.

You, and all those other persons may simply be directionally challenged. I am also a directionally challenged individual. Being directionally challenged is not gender-specific, neither is it peculiar to a specific cultural or ethnic group, and it's a characteristic found in individuals the world over!

As directionally challenged individuals, we have varying degrees of difficulty identifying right from left, and the points on a compass. This can make it difficult for us to identify where we are in relation to other persons, or objects around us. While some people have a natural ability to understand and remember directions, directionally challenged individuals, like us, struggle.

What's your take on this?

Last year, a young man from England - let's call him John - traveled to Paris for the first time. Despite having a map, a guidebook and his cell phone, John struggled to navigate the city's winding streets and complex metro system. He attempted to visit landmarks like the Eiffel Tower and the Louvre but found himself constantly disoriented. At one point, he got on the wrong train and ended up in a suburb far from the city center where he was staying. Frustrated and unable to find his way, he had to rely on his voice translator and the kindness of locals, to guide him back to his hotel. For the rest of his visit, John relied on taxi cabs.

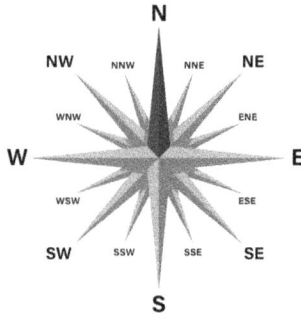

The truth is, some of us who are directionally challenged, can easily identify east, west, north and south, yet they struggle with distinguishing right from left. For others, the reverse is true, while there are still others who are challenged in both areas. I happen to be challenged in both areas.

But the difficulty in navigating between people, objects and locations does not mean that directionally challenged individuals are less intelligent than anyone else. It just means that our brains process spatial information differently. We perceive the world in a unique way.

What may seem to be simple tasks undertaken by those who are spatially adept can be overwhelming for us.

Many directionally challenged individuals will admit to avoiding or delaying the task of learning to drive, or, never learning to drive. Even those who manage to obtain their drivers' licenses, really dread taking road trips. In my case, despite holding a Learner's Permit in Jamaica, for decades, I never felt ready to take the driver's test.

After moving to the United States, I realized that I had no choice but to obtain a driver's license. In the final year of the 20th century, I visited the DMV in Fort Lauderdale, Florida. The written portion of the test was a breeze, but the driving test? Let's just say it didn't go as planned.

The examiner got into the front passenger seat and instructed me to reverse. That, to me, was anathema, because I had never fully mastered reversing. I started that car, put it in reverse and pressed the gas. I don't know what happened next, but I noticed that the examiner had become as white as a sheet. I glanced out the window, and realized that I was on the wrong side of the road— the left side! Thank God there were no vehicles approaching.

It was only much later on, when I decided to teach myself to reverse, that I was able to achieve any competence at this skill. It took time, but I talked my way through it. Once I could get the instructions right in my head, and could repeat to myself, "It's just like forward driving, but forward driving in reverse," I could reverse.

However, even now, I wouldn't claim to be competent at reversing, but I've mastered a solid three-point turn. What I can't do, and frankly have no desire to learn to do, is parallel park in a big city where the space you're expected to squeeze into is barely the length of your vehicle!

Are you like me?

"I can best describe how I feel by saying that even in an area I know well, it's like my brain does a 'factory reset' and suddenly everything is completely unfamiliar." - Chris P.

Directionally challenged individuals are different. We see things differently and we think differently.

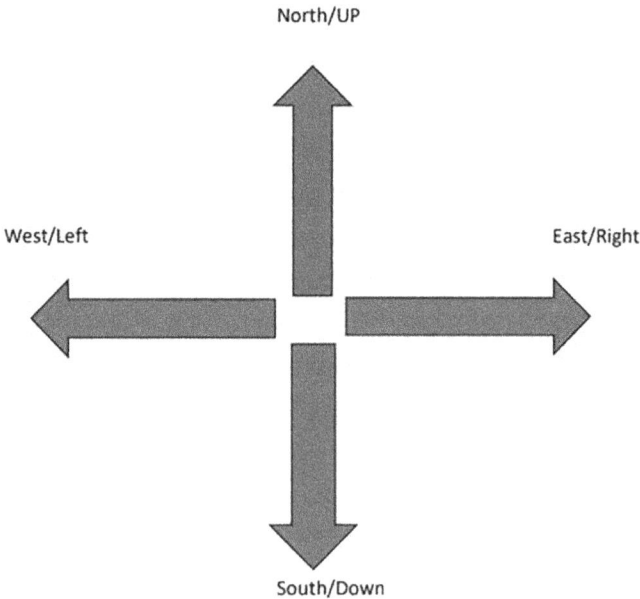

North/UP

West/Left

East/Right

South/Down

I am most comfortable with "here," "there," "this way," "that way," "up" and "down." It's so much easier for me to use hand gestures when I speak about direction. Instead of saying something or someone is to my right or left, I point. I sometimes use 'here' or 'this way' as opposed to 'there' or 'that way' to identify distance. However, most of the time, to me, "here" or "this way" is simply the one I mentioned first. As regards the cardinal points, I am completely intimidated. Even though I acknowledge that the sun rises in the east, to me, it appears that the east can be in different positions, depending on where I am. To get a rough idea of east to west, I try to spend some time observing the movement of the sun. If I'm able to accurately pinpoint east and west, I can usually work out where north and south are. The challenge is that most times I do not have the time, so I guess.

Interestingly, I'm not one to be at a location that is clearly identified as "south" on a map, and say that I'm going "down" to another location that is clearly identified as being in the "north'" on the same map, or vice versa. But I know many people like that!

However, as someone who resided between Church Avenue and Flatbush Junction, in Brooklyn, New York, in the United States, it seemed perfectly logical to me to say that I was going down to Church Avenue, and up to Flatbush Junction. My husband "corrected" me on every occasion.

We had running debates not just about where was up and where was down, but also about why what he said was up, was up, and not what I said, was up. He said things like Church Avenue was to our north, and therefore it was up, while Flatbush Junction was to our south, and therefore it was down. He insisted that water should flow from Church Avenue (which was up, to him), (down) to the Flatbush Junction.

On the other hand, for my inspiration, I looked at the numerous vehicles parked on our street. I was not prepared to venture to say which direction was north and which was south. I was more concerned with which way was up and which was down.

If the vehicles were facing Flatbush Junction, they appeared, to me, to be slanted, with the front appearing higher than the back, therefore, Church Avenue was "down" from Flatbush Junction. The fact that, one hot summer day, someone opened a fire hydrant on East 34th Street, and the water ran from Snyder Avenue, to Church Avenue supported my position. Based on what my husband said, that was water running south to north. All I saw was water running "down" to Church Avenue.

This vehicle was parked with the front towards the Flatbush Junction. To me, the back of the vehicle appeared lower than the front.

But the story of the those who cannot navigate spatially is important! I do know that a few books have been written, mostly by academicians or scientists, who give their perspectives on the directionally challenged. However, I am here to expose to the rest of the world, the perceptions of those who have severe difficulty identifying directions; to highlight what exactly goes on in the minds of persons who cannot tell left from right, east from west or north from south, many of whom are brilliant in almost all other ways. My hope is that my exposé of what we experience will bring recognition and validation to our predicament. I also anticipate that any and all allowance that can be made, to accommodate and facilitate our situation, will be granted.

The first step in solving any problem is to have a good grasp of what the problem entails. For the next few chapters, therefore, we'll examine the nuances of our being directionally challenged.

2
The challenge of the directionally confused

"For most of my life I didn't want to volunteer to be the driver for even a simple trip of going to lunch with coworkers because I didn't want to get embarrassed about not knowing how to get to the restaurant." - DLC

"DLC, I was most adept at leaving my car in my garage, and thumbing a lift. The problem was, on our way back, I'd be unable to give proper directions to the driver about how to get to my own home!" - EPG

Being directionally challenged is tough. I know that. You know that. The truth is, though, those who have no difficulty finding their way have not even the faintest idea what we experience on a daily basis. Not only do we have to negotiate a world that appears very complicated to us, but we constantly have to make excuses for what others characterize as inattentiveness, or forgetfulness, carelessness or even a disability.

THE EVERYDAY TRIALS OF YOUNG IONA

On a small little tropical island, there lived a girl named Iona Frezzinski. She lived with her grandmother in a rural section of the island, but she often went to spend the weekend with her mother, in a town on the other side of the island. Everyone who knew her, concluded that Ionia was highly intelligent and responsible for her age. That was one of the reasons her mom and grandmother were comfortable about placing her on the lone bus that traveled the route between where they both lived, expecting that she could take care of herself, and get off at the correct stops. Another reason, of course, is that this happened during a much gentler era, when more adults tended to be protective of unaccompanied minors.

At her grandmother's home, little Ionia would often awaken to the early morning sunlight on her cheeks, as its rays beamed through the glass panes of the tiny window over her bed. Iona knew that the sun rose in the east, so she figured that her bed faced the east, and that was fine.

There was a problem, however, when Ionia slept at her mom's house. From her perspective, the street and her mom's house were similarly aligned to how the road and her grand-mother's house were aligned. Why, then did it appear, at her mom's house, that the sun rose in what Ioni thought was the west; and set in what she thought was the east? No number of explanations from her mom, her grandmother, her uncles and aunts, could dissuade Ionia from asserting that east was one direction at her grandma's, and another direction at her mom's.

Truth be told, Ionia had other challenges. Notwithstanding the fact that she was known to be very conscientious, her grandmother would often become extremely impatient with her when she spent an inordinately long time on any errand on which she was sent. Yes, the village more or less had only one main road, with several little avenues deviating from it, but that did not prevent Ionia from being totally confused about which direction to take, after exiting one of the little pathways. She would usually point and say, "Eenie, eenie, minie, moh. Catch a tiger by its toe. If you ever let it go, eenie, eenie, minie, moh! ..." and choose the direction to which she was pointing, when she said the last "moh." Many times, she chose the wrong direction, and it was only after being convinced that she was definitely going the wrong way, that she would turn around and head in the opposite direction. When her grandma asked, "What took you so long?" Ionia would mutter some excuse. She was too embarrassed to say that she had been lost! Of course, it was worse in the town where her mother lived.

Now, when traveling to her mother's house, Ionia always sat in the third row from the front, on the driver's side of the vehicle. Even if the seat was occupied when she first got on, Iona would stand close by, or wait until its occupant got off and then she would claim what she saw as her seat. From this vantage point, she had a great view of the road ahead. She would know that she was near her stop, when she saw a large lot, with several abandoned motor vehicles on her side of the road. She could readily identify the various abandoned vehicles. She also knew, on her way back to her grandmother's, that she should ask the bus driver to stop, when she reached the area where two large mango trees grew on either side of the road, and almost touched each other, forming a near perfect arch over the roadway.

However, when her mother sent her to the store, which was a few blocks from her house, Ionia was traumatized. On the first occasion, her mother had carefully directed, "Turn left when you exit the gate, then turn right at the corner. Go for two more blocks and make a left at the end of the second block. You'll see two stores facing each other. Go to the one on the right." How could poor Ionia follow such instructions? She didn't know her right hand from her left hand! It took many, many trials and failures for her to discover that the store "on the right," to which her mom sent her, had a huge cardboard effigy of Superman on one side. So, knowing which store to enter became a cinch – as long as Superman remained there. However, getting to that particular intersection was not so easy. Then, after she made her purchase, getting back home was another nightmare! To travel between her place of abode, and the store, Ionia often took several turns which seemed to lead her further and further away from both her starting point and her destination. Sometimes, she would have to retrace her steps and return to a point that was familiar, even if it was the gate of her mother's yard or the front of the store she had just visited, then start the journey all over.

But it's not just Iona

If you think that Ionia was just a simple child, let's consider the case of the renowned neurologist, Dr. Oliver Sacks. Despite his intellectual prowess and his groundbreaking work in the field of neurology, the epitome of the "absent-minded professor" or the "nerd," Dr. Sacks was notoriously bad at finding his way around. In one of his memoirs, "On the Move", he confessed to having a terrible sense of direction and, to often getting lost in his own neighborhood. He would frequently end up in the wrong place, despite having lived in the same area for years. His condition was so severe that he even got lost in his own home. However, don't feel sorry for Dr. Sacks. Despite his propensity for losing his way, he was able to have a successful career and make significant contributions to his field.

Although I am definitely not in Dr. Sacks' league in terms of academic or other achievements, I am certainly not the dimmest bulb in the socket. But I too, can attest to becoming lost and totally disoriented, on my way to and from work on many occasions. It goes without saying, therefore, that my road trip to an unfamiliar destination would be sheer trauma. Yes, a global positioning system (GPS) does help, but GPS seems unable to account for the fact that I will need to make any stops, and in its effort to get me back on the route, it will totally confuse me.

Before there was GPS, I would be absolutely terrified that I could re-enter the roadway, going in the wrong direction. The main problems I now experience occur during those times when the GPS gives me sudden instructions.

However, even if I miss the exit – and that happens often, I've learned not to be flustered – and do something silly. I simply continue driving until the GPS redirects me. You will understand why, if I have to make a long trip on the highway, I calculate at least one extra hour into my commute, just for making detours, and getting back on the prescribed route. You will also understand why, for me, a quarter tank of petrol is my Empty. I cannot allow my tank to run dry, as I wend my way through endless unknown alleys. Again, you will understand when I tell you that my GPS has learned my idiosyncrasies. Whenever I type in a strange destination, it automatically directs me to the back roads, because it now knows that I avoid highways if I can.

I must say this, though, and perhaps you can identify with this too. Because I know all the processes that go on in my head when I have to drive on the highway or even when I have to drive on the streets in my little town, I am most considerate towards other people who do silly stuff while driving. The explanation for my attitude is simple. I do silly stuff when I'm on the road, not because I'm a road hog; not because I'm malicious in any way. It's because I am so out of my comfort zone when I am driving. Case in point about being out of my depth: I once took a trip on I-95, from Fort Lauderdale to Boynton Beach and back - a round trip of just under 90 kilometers (60 miles). I was so tense the entire time, that I developed extremely painful muscle cramps that lasted for days and almost crippled me! I was worried stiff that I would not be able to walk properly ever again. Of course, I now know that it was lactic acid being produced in my muscles because they were ALL contracted the entire time! And because my breathing was so restricted, I was extremely low on oxygen! What my body experienced on that trip would be similar to what a runner would go through, if he or she did a 5-mile marathon in a high-altitude location, without any preparation at all. No wonder I did something really stupid on that trip. I'll tell you about it later.

So, directionally challenged individuals do experience difficulties navigating from one place to another. We might excel in most tests or in our chosen fields, but we all seem to have one trait in common. We are inept in finding locations, after being given the directions, or even after traveling to those places several times.

There are even moments when we get lost in a building, whether it's a large office or a department store. I once lived in rural Western North Carolina, near to a town that prides itself on being small. Needless to say, the townsfolk weren't thrilled when a super-sized store opened in the area, and that was understandable, because that store caused the closure of not just scores of "mom & pop" shops, but also the local branches of more than a few large chain stores.

But I had a friend who had a particular disdain this new store. One day, as I urged her to tell me why she was so against even visiting it, after giving me a number of plausible reasons, she finally admitted that the one time she had visited the store, she was completely overwhelmed by its size. After she entered it, she said, she actually could not find the right exit to leave the store! "Do you know how embarrassing it was to have to call a member of my family and ask them to come and fetch me?" she wailed.

I didn't have the heart to tell her that I, too, had been lost in big stores – not in that particular store, but others. And, of course, if the store is huge, chances are, the parking lot is massive! And it will have several exits! To top it off, after searching for my vehicle for a really long time, with my luck, I will finally locate it, and then exit onto a street I have never seen before! At least, that's how it will appear to me!

Speaking of large buildings, I've worked for years in schools, and a hospital. Knowing my directional challenge, I always gave myself extra time to get to my post. At the hospital, I'd linger near the entrance, until I saw someone to walk with, to the clock-in area. I usually worked in one small section, so I managed there, fairly well. But if I was called to help out in another department? Let's just say that I was not going to get there quickly!

I also worked as a substitute teacher; therefore, I was at a different school almost every day. If I was assigned to one room, and the students came to me each session, things would be fine. If I had to travel to different classrooms, sometimes the students had to come looking for me! And, finding the restroom, then navigating my way back to a classroom was also fraught with difficulty! If I was placed in charge of very young children, I had to escort them to various locations - the music room, the computer room, the gym, the cafeteria, etc. I had the children with me as I took them to the different rooms, and they knew the way, so thing went well. Close to the end of the session, when I had to go back to get them, I would experience real angst, trying to navigate the maze of corridors and staircases.

It is fortunate that many persons can now work from home This is a tremendous relief for those of us who are able to avoid the commute. But not all of us can avoid driving to work, or navigating large office buildings. So, we struggle daily to do tasks that others do without even thinking. These tasks include reaching for an object that is to our right or left, pointing to the east, west, north or south and navigating from point A to point B. Many of us may permanently feel lost. I do not permanently feel lost, but I have this sensation often enough to know that I am not like others who have no challenge navigating even if the directions are very complicated. Therefore, we need to delve a little deeper, to try to decipher why there's this big difference in our experiences. That's what we'll do in the next chapter.

3
Hand or side dominance - What is that?

One question that has intrigued me for a very long time is, how people became either right-handed or left-handed. It seems that hand dominance may mostly be a learned trait, and over time, one hand simply became the preferred one to use. Another question is, does hand-dominance affect our ability to navigate? I badly needed answers, so, I did some research.

What I found is that, for many years, scientists and researchers have been concerned about what causes people to be left-handed or right-handed, but the whole notion of handedness is still mysterious. The truth is, no one human is truly right-handed or left-handed. We all tend to use both hands to do most things, even if the efforts of one hand may be stronger or feebler than the other.

It's not really known when humans first began to show a dominance on one side. Having a dominant side means using the limbs on that side to do most tasks - writing, tossing, hopping, kicking, etc., etc. Interestingly, excavated Stone Age tools suggest that people may have trended towards left-handedness in that era, while tools discovered and thought to belong to later periods show a clear shift to right-handedness. Dominance also extends to sense organs such as the eyes and ears. For example, if you instinctively cup your right ear, or turn you head to the right, to hear better, your right ear is dominant. Likewise, if a sudden bright light flashes and you close your eyes, the eye that closes first is your weaker eye. Your dominant eye is the one that opens first, as you reopen them. At present, it's a common belief, that roughly 80 percent of all humans are right-side dominant, meaning they use the limbs and organs on their right most of the time.

Don't be dismayed, however, if you find that you have a dominant left eye and a dominant right hand, or a dominant left hand and a dominant right ear. Actually, one ear or eye may not be dominant at all. These things do happen. We'll explore that later.

About 15 percent of all humans have a dominant left hand, while there is a five percent or so that is ambidextrous. I think I've met only one person who I believe is truly ambidextrous. The truly ambidextrous - a really rare group - is able to do a great job, on any task, with either hand!

It is believed that a complex interplay of genetics and environment, determines hand- and side-dominance, with genetics playing a more significant role. Studies have shown that handedness tends to run in families, with just a few outliers. Several members of a family may be right-handed, or most of them may be left-handed. However, we still don't know the exact genes involved. There really isn't a single "left-handed gene" or a "right-handed gene," but instead, multiple genes contribute to handedness.

The environment in which one is nurtured is also significant. For example, studies have suggested that the position of the fetus in the womb can influence which hand becomes dominant for the child. Also, the way the infant is held in the arms of a caregiver can promote or hinder its use of either hand. If a baby is held on the lap or in the arms of an adult, and one of his or her arms is constantly positioned either behind the adult, or squeezed between the bodies of the child and the adult, the child will only have one hand that he or she can freely move. That hand will be used to hold the breast or bottle, while feeding, or to hold a toy or pacifier. With continuous use of that hand while in that position, the child is likely to more actively use that hand in later life, regardless of whether the child is left-brained or right-brained.

HOW TO HOLD A BABY

Incorrect way to hold a baby.

Correct way to hold a baby.
CREDIT: Colorfuel Studio

Many adults are careful to allow the free movement of both arms of the baby being held, but this is not always the case. Besides, how the baby is held depends on the handedness of the adult holding the baby incorrectly. If the person holding the baby improperly, is left-handed, it is likely that the child's right hand may be out of commission, and the left hand will be free, and vice versa. In addition to the genetic factor, therefore, that practice can also account for the fact that handedness runs in families.

We do know that it is our brains that determine much of whatever we do, so we need to know a little about the brain.

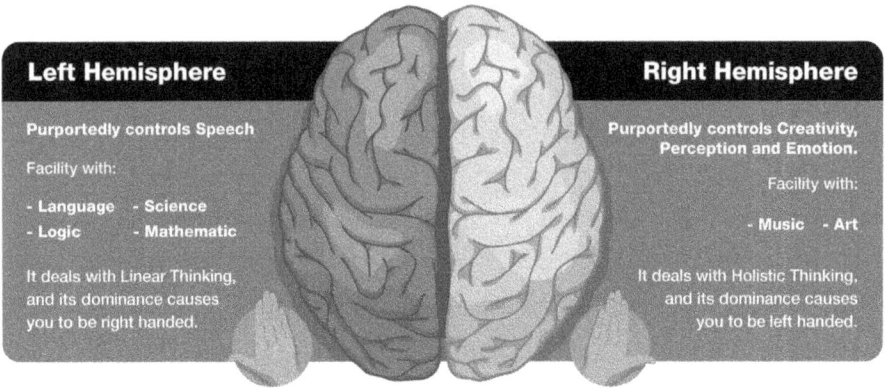

Left Hemisphere	Right Hemisphere
Purportedly controls Speech	Purportedly controls Creativity, Perception and Emotion.
Facility with:	Facility with:
- Language - Science	- Music - Art
- Logic - Mathematic	
It deals with Linear Thinking, and its dominance causes you to be right handed.	It deals with Holistic Thinking, and its dominance causes you to be left handed.

Brain Hemispheres

Physiologists divide the brain into two almost symmetrical sides called hemispheres. There is a right hemisphere and a left hemisphere. The two hemispheres purportedly are each responsible for different cognitive functions. A dominant right hemisphere seems to make a person left-handed, and a dominant left hemisphere may make him or her right-handed. Some experts believe that the left hemisphere is associated with logical thinking, analytical processes, and accuracy, while the right hemisphere is linked to creativity, imagination, and intuition. This doesn't mean that one hemisphere is superior to the other or that they carry out their functions independently. Both hemispheres are equally important and contribute to our overall cognitive abilities.

It is true that circumstances can cause someone to transfer dominance from one hand to the other. Injury to the dominant hand, or side of the brain, is a leading reason many persons, especially adults, will change their handedness. Also, many persons affected by strokes and other illnesses that permanently damage one hemisphere of their brains, may, through physical and occupational therapy, be trained to transfer dominance to the uninjured hemisphere.

HANDEDNESS AND SPATIAL NAVIGATION

One early researcher into the question of how our handedness affects our perspectives was Daniel Casasanto. His studies found that both concrete perceptions and abstract thoughts could be controlled by neuronal circuits. As a postdoctoral scholar in Psychology, at Sanford University, Casasanto coined what he called the Body-Specific Hypothesis, in which he showed that different physical characteristics, such as handedness, could strongly determine the abstract consciousness of persons (Casasanto, 2011). There is certainly the need for a better understanding of the perspectives of those whose handedness differs from that of the majority, especially as we consider whether forcing someone to change his or her handedness could affect his or her ability to navigate. This is a theory that definitely needs more exploration.

So, how can you determine whether you're right- or left-handed?

I believe something extraordinary happens when a right-handed person is told an item is to their right side. In just nanoseconds, multiple processes take place within the person. The body asks, "Which side is my right side?" This question is relayed to the brain. The brain wires back: 'It's your dominant side." Because the person instinctively knows which side is dominant – the side they use for most activities – it is quite easy for them to turn to their right, and locate the object. The same thing happens if a left-handed person is told that the item is to his/her left. Likewise, if a right-handed person is told the object is to their left, or, a left-handed person is told the object is to their right, after the same processes, the brain will guide the person to turn to their non-dominant or weaker side.

I believe utter confusion arises when, due to various factors, a glitch occurs in these mental processes. In such cases, the brain struggles to determine dominance, and the person may be unable to navigate in such a situation.

I do not appear to have a dominant side! I'll go more into that in a later chapter, but, as I did the research for this book, I came across a plethora of theories on handedness. I also submitted myself to many of the left-handed/right-handed tests available online. The most interesting one I found was on a left-handers' webpage, at https://www.left-handersday.com/tour9.html.

This test declares, "Because their brains are organized differently, left-handers see and think differently and can get some very different results from various 'brain tests,' usually doing well on tests that involve creative thinking or unraveling complex images and manipulating 3D images" (Lefthandersday.com).

It involves a picture displayed in a series of black and white blots. The creators of the test assert that a left-brained, right-handed person will only see "a hodgepodge of disconnected shapes, but the right-brained, left-handed person can go beyond logic, and find the connecting concept that makes sense of the shapes." According to this website if you cannot see beyond the random shapes, "it's because your right-handed brain is trying to solve the problem and won't let your left-handed brain have a go" (Ibid).

I won't disclose the answer to the test, as I urge you to visit the page and try it, I will say, though, that the result I achieved was in keeping with my understanding about myself. I was readily able to identify a good portion of the picture, but certain aspects really appeared as "only a hodgepodge of disconnected shapes." This test, and others I did seem to confirm I am neither totally left-brain- nor totally right-brain-dominant.

Other research shows cultural and societal factors can also influence handedness. For instance, in some cultures, children are encouraged or even forced to use their right hand, even if they naturally prefer to use their left hand. This is why some people will only *appear* to be right-handed. In their formative years, they were trending towards left-handedness, but because of whatever circumstance, they made a shift, at least in some of the functions carried out by the hands - writing being the main one.

In the Caribbean, where I'm from, left-handed persons were often referred to as "baff-handed." The Caribbean Dictionary on X (formerly Twitter) describes baff-handedness as "Clumsy. Lacking in grace or dexterity. Awkward or prone to accidents" - #Jamaica https://t.co/EdflLRrPUQ.

Many Caribbean parents, not wanting their children to be described as "baff-handed," would use various methods to "encourage" their children to use their right hand. My mother was one such parent. She insisted that no child of hers would become left-handed (baff-handed) if she could help it. Her methods were more coercive than creative, but definitely persuasive.

I must also say, however, that the apparent clumsiness of many left-handers can be traced to the fact that they have had to use equipment and tools made by right-handers, for right-handers. Many left-handers struggle because almost everything is oriented towards right-handedness. For example, in class-rooms where the chair and desk are a single unit, they are almost always designed for right-handed students. A left-handed child has to twist awkwardly to write at such a desk. For this reason, many unenlightened teachers would force children to write with their right hand. However, if a right-brain-dominant child is forced to use their right hand, can you imagine how confused they can become when determining the location of objects to their right or left side? Now you can see a reason for many of the trials of the directionally challenged.

Sociocultural bias against left-handers is not confined to the Caribbean but exists in many locations around the world. This bias may be rooted, at least in part, in Judeo-Islamic-Christian principles. The holy books of these religions contain numerous references to the right side being associated with righteousness and the left side being undesirable. Ironically, the scientific research on handedness suggests that if you are left-handed, the right hemisphere of your brain is dominant, and vice versa!

By the way, did you know the English word "left" is derived from a term that once meant "sinister?" These early designators were clearly biased against the left!

The good news is that left-handedness, once stigmatized and thought of as sinister, is now widely accepted and recognized as a natural variation in human behavior. Left-handers are celebrated for their creativity, talent, and leadership qualities. Think of notable left-handers like Albert Einstein, Leonardo da Vinci, Ludwig van Beethoven, Benjamin Franklin, John McEnroe, and Bill Clinton.

William "Bill" Clinton was the 42nd president of the United States. At least seven U.S. presidents have been left-handers, and there were at least two others who wrote with their left hand after injuries to their right hand. While it's not clear how many of these brilliant left-handed individuals faced challenges with direction or navigation, a common comment in the United States used to be, "You have a very good chance of becoming president!" whenever an adult met a left-handed child.

AM I DIRECTIONALLY CHALLENGED BECAUSE I'M ____ HANDED?

On an average day, how many right-handed individuals, compared to left-handed individuals do you encounter? Among them, how many do you think are directionally challenged? Why does a significant portion of the human race experience varying degrees of difficulty with spatial navigation? Could it be that during our early developmental years, the processes crucial for differentiating right from left and for spatial navigation were somehow interrupted?

You may be aware that, like many others, I am directionally challenged. But do you think there is a connection between my handedness and my directional confusion? While the jury is still out on whether handedness affects spatial cognition, it is possible that our confusion on the road is influenced by the way road signs are constructed, and travel directions are given, which often seem to cater to right-handers. However, this cannot be the complete explanation, since many right-handers also experience difficulty navigating both familiar and unfamiliar territories. Clearly, more research is needed in this area.

Being directionally challenged may often—but not always—indicate a brain that leans more towards the right hemisphere's functions. This may mean that we are more creative, intuitive, and imaginative, but struggle with spatial tasks associated with the left hemisphere's functions, like navigating or remembering directions. However, it's important to note that someone can be directionally challenged while still being logical and analytical. Think of the proverbial absent-minded professor. Maybe we're logical and analytical in some areas, but not in others.

MEET THE CORPUS CALLOSUM

There is considerable debate regarding the autonomy of each hemisphere, their influence on handedness, and the impact of handedness on our navigational abilities. Furthermore, the relationship between interactions of the hemispheres, and our capacity to navigate remains a complex topic. The two hemispheres are interconnected by the corpus callosum, the thick bundle of nerve fibers consisting of over two hundred million axons. Previously unfamiliar to me, I now understand the critical role these cranial connectors play. The corpus callosum functions as a bridge, enabling the seamless exchange of information between the two hemispheres.

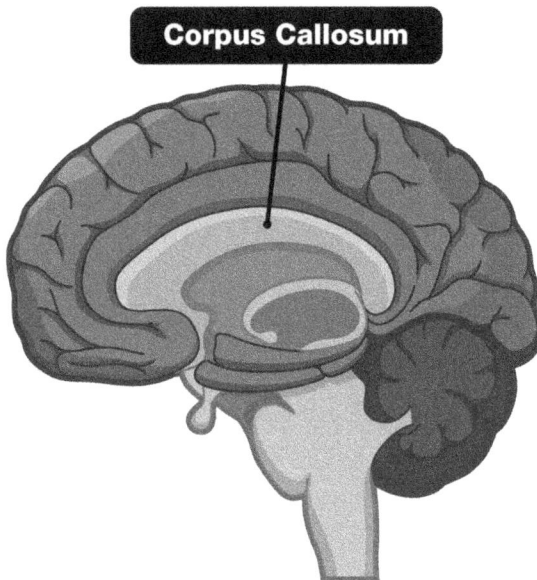

Corpus Callosum

In the mid-1950s, scientists discovered that the primary role of the corpus callosum involves coordination, and complex problem-solving. Remarkably, individuals can be born without a corpus callosum, or with an underdeveloped one, a condition known as agenesis of the corpus callosum (ACC). Additionally, the corpus callosum can be surgically removed, either partially or completely. It was during the early to mid-1900s that medical science began experiments to sever the connection between the two hemispheres by splitting or removing portions of the corpus callosum, primarily as a treatment for severe epilepsy.

IS DIRECTIONAL CHALLENGE CONGENITAL OR LEARNED?

Whether the corpus callosum is surgically removed or missing from birth, its absence results in significant coordinational difficulties, and a degree of competition between the two hemispheres. This absence can lead to various cognitive challenges, including difficulty reading facial expressions or voice tones, problem solving, handling complex tasks, assessing risks, understanding abstract concepts, interpreting slang or sarcasm, and comprehending emotions. ACC may even cause a tendency to disseminate false information. This is no joke.

The importance of the corpus callosum becomes evident when tackling complex tasks such as navigating through a maze of rooms in a large building or finding your way along any street—familiar or not. This information about the corpus callosum causes me to ask these questions: Is *my* corpus callosum functioning optimally? Is it effectively transmitting and coordinating information between the two hemispheres in *my* brain, or is there a blockage causing each hemisphere to operate independently?

Much remains to be known about side dominance and handedness, the comprehensive functions of the brain's hemispheres, and how their interaction influences our navigational abilities. However, if there is dysfunction, the apparent discord between the hemispheres could be the underlying issue for many who experience spatial disorientation.

WHAT WAS SHE THINKING?

I'm sure my mother believed she was acting in my best interest when she would punish me for writing with my left hand, and reward me when I used my right hand. The truth is, I wasn't attempting to favor my left hand for writing, especially since, at the time, I couldn't distinguish between my left and right hands. It felt natural for me to use both hands interchangeably. However, my mother was adamantly opposed to my left-handed writing. This eventually led me to abandon any effort to write with my left hand. Note that I could still perform several other activities effectively with my left hand, and some with both hands. My mother didn't seem to mind this, as long as I wrote with my right hand. I believe her actions forced my brain to neglect one aspect of my handedness while over-emphasizing the other, potentially contributing to my difficulty in instinctively identifying my dominant or weaker hand.

This brings to the floor, an important question: How many people who currently use their right hand to do most tasks were actually forced to switch their hand dominance? If this number is significant, we must also consider whether this scenario is reflected in the number of individuals who struggle to identify their right or left side and those who have difficulty navigating from one point to another. To gain clarity on these perspectives, further research is essential. We need to delve deeper into the experiences of individuals who frequently face directional confusion, regardless of whether they are right-handed, left-handed, or ambidextrous. This exploration will continue in the next chapter.

4
What is happening to us?

"I carried written directions from my house to town and
back, for two years, after moving to a new town."
—Diane V.

DIRECTIONAL CONFUSION

Have you ever given someone directions and then worried yourself sick about how they fared if they followed your suggestions? I do that sometimes, but not too often. Most times when

I'm asked for directions, I'll simply say, "I'm sorry. I haven't got the slightest idea." But there are occasions when I'll actually provide directions. Mind you, it won't be the usual set of instructions like "Turn right at the next intersection, go four blocks, then turn left," etc. Instead, I'll say something like, "Go to the next corner and turn this way," motioning with either hand, "then continue for another two or three blocks and turn down the next avenue. Proceed until you see a huge billboard with a football team on it. (You know those things are temporary, but it was there the last time I passed that way.) Turn that way," motioning with one hand again, "and the address you're looking for should be in the middle of that block." Like I said, I don't give travel advisories often, but I do worry about the fate of anyone who followed my directions.

I'm also quite relieved that most of the people who gave me driving directions didn't stick around to see me "follow" their instructions. If I'm in an unfamiliar place, trying to navigate to another location, strange or familiar, it causes me a good deal of stress because I won't even know how to make the first turn. If I cannot decipher the way and I ask for directions, somebody may say, "Go to the next block and turn right. And then, when you get there..." I'll thank them, and move on, but later on I'll wonder, "Did the person say to first turn right or turn left?" I'll be challenged to decode the instructions even before I try to decipher which direction is right and which is left. Nowadays, if I'm driving and even if I'm walking, GPS can be helpful. I have a better chance of finding my way when I follow the arrows on the GPS app. It doesn't just say, "Turn right." It actually points in the direction where right is. It's a challenge for me though, to drive and keep glancing at the GPS app. So, I still have issues, even with GPS.

In addition, I cannot count the number of times that I have gotten lost while walking in absolutely familiar territory. And I did say, walking. Walking is safer than driving for me, but it is not fail-safe because I remember so many times, I would get to my street, and the houses would look so strange that if I were not looking for numbers, or if there were no outstanding landmarks, it is likely that I could have passed my own house. Numbers and outstanding landmarks are very important for me, because sometimes they're all I have to prevent me from being completely lost in familiar territory. Sometimes, it is one single item in a sea of strange objects that will help me to recognize where I am. While I've never actually passed my house, many times I have passed the houses of friends, places I had visited several times before.

But here's another question: Are you comfortable with the interval at which your GPS gives you instructions? I'm not. It will say, "In half a mile turn left onto Pyzer Street." or "In four hundred feet turn, right." Even though the distance is counting down on the app, I am not seeing that because I am looking straight ahead. I'm always surprised when the app suddenly says, "Turn left!" or "Turn right!" Almost invariably, it says it when I'm parallel with the exit, although I thought I had a few more "feet" left! I could be past the exit by the time I process the command. Therefore, I don't know if it is just with my GPS or GPSs generally, but there just seems to be a timing issue. When I'm alone and using it, I seem to be always screaming, "Why didn't you say that a minute or two earlier?"

Here are other ways my directional confusion manifests itself: Not only am I not able to follow directions correctly, but if I happen to veer off course, then have to turn around, on some narrow lane, and reversing is involved, I may be in a spot of trouble, because I have always had such a difficulty using the rearview mirror to reverse! But, speaking of mirrors, do you also have difficulty with a mirror? When I was a child, it was impossible for me to use a mirror to fix my hair, or do something to my face! When I tried to touch the left side of my face, while looking in the mirror, my hand would end up on the right side. To this day, although I do a bit better now, it is still a challenge for me to use the mirror to touch a particular spot on my face. What is that?

To turn or not to turn?

I have not always lived in areas where there are numbers on the buildings or in towns or cities where the blocks are laid out precisely. In some of these city areas, one store on any corner will look exactly like the store on another corner. That situation is challenging in and of itself, but when, like me, you have lived in rural areas where the most common repetitive objects are trees, you know we have to use different methods to navigate, and many times our efforts are not successful.

Have you been given directions that included turning right or left at the "fork in the road?" How did that go? As for me, in cases like these, I spend precious time contemplating what really constitutes the "fork," and thinking, 'Should I look for a two-pronged fork or a three- or four-pronged fork?' I would have to complete that assessment *before* trying to decipher which road was on the left or right! I tell you, following directions is not my forte.

Negotiating ramps and turning lanes

I mentioned before, my journey from Fort Lauderdale to Boynton Beach and back – in Florida, on I-95 –, and how petrified I was the entire time. But there was also an incident (I alluded to it earlier) in which I was in the right lane, and there was a vehicle merging onto the highway. I looked at my rearview mirror, and I saw another vehicle right behind me, and another, in the middle lane, some distance away. I indicated, and quickly changed lanes. The vehicle that was then behind me, sped up with its horn blaring. The driver then shifted over to the left lane, sped past me, and as he did, he swore at me. I was so intimidated! To this day, I'm not sure what I did to earn his ire. But I accept that whatever it was, I was wrong, because I know that I don't change lanes well. I just don't like ramps on highways.

I don't merge onto the highway well, either. There have been times when I've tried to merge and was pushed off the road, because apparently there wasn't enough distance between the vehicle traveling in the right lane and my vehicle. Some people are just road hogs, I guess, because I also remember a time, when, as I was merging onto I-74, in North Carolina, I saw this man coming in a pick-up with a trailer attached. I know my road depth perception is not the best, but there was no other vehicle on the road, so, I just assumed that he would have switched lanes to allow me to enter. He didn't. I had to quickly swerve because he almost ran me over. Like I said, I don't like highways. I also try my best to avoid roundabouts. If a roundabout is unavoidable, I mentally prepare myself for using it the number of options it offers. Sometimes I get it right the second or third time - never the first!

Driving takes every bit of my concentration. That is the major reason I do not take or make calls, or worse, text, while I'm driving! I happen to have a "SAFE DRIVER" designation on my driver's license, and I am "safe" where those habits are concerned, but not for the usual reasons – "Arrive Alive! Don't text and drive!" When I drive, driving is all I *can* do.

Who else?

Here is what Sharon Whitfield, a member of an online support group for the directionally challenged had to say:

> *"When traveling a so called, known or local journey, my struggle can mean the middle of the journey is sometimes not there. That means there's no connection between the beginning and the final destination of the journey.*
>
> *If I drive a satnav [vehicle with satellite navigation] it certainly helps, and it's so much easier than many years ago when I was embarrassed trying to direct a friend to my house, when they offered me a lift home from a local place.*
>
> *Being directionally challenged is like being a tourist in your own town most times, and the constant fear and panic that says, 'I'm lost and I have no idea where to go!'*
>
> *I actually used to get lost in school at times, trying to find certain classrooms.*
> *I could go on forever! I'm so passionate about this!"*

Rainy nights and days

I moved to rural North Carolina in the middle of winter. I had just started getting used to the landscape, when spring came, and everything changed. It did not matter that I had been driving on those roads for a few months. The fact that I could no longer see a good distance ahead, because of the thick foliage that had quickly appeared, caused me to pass my exit on many, many occasions.

Whatever navigational prowess I have (non-existent as that is) totally disappears, if it gets dark OR it starts to rain. If both of them happen at the same time, I'm pulling off the road and staying put! I do this even though experience has taught me that, especially in Florida, there is no rain half a mile from where it's raining cats and dogs.

I worked nights - the "grave-yard" shift - for several years. It was relatively easy to get to work because I traveled one lonely country road, to the interstate highway, and the next town, where I worked, was only two exits away. However, if it was raining, as was often the case, it was a nightmare to get to work. I could not distinguish between the road and the curb; and I could not find the exits!

One night as I drove down my driveway to the road, I saw huge flashes of lightning in the sky, in the direction I would be taking, but I didn't give much thought to it. I was driving along, quite content with the time I had to get to work and my general wellbeing... Suddenly I rounded a deep corner and ran into one of the most violent storms I have ever experienced! I was totally blinded and my car slowed to a literal crawl. I turned my caution lights on, just to alert other drivers that I did not know what I was doing. In fact, a distance that normally took me ten to fifteen minutes to cover, took close to an hour, and I doubt that I would have made it, had not a very kind big rig driver come up behind me, once I managed to get onto the highway, and used his headlights to guide me. The irony was that once I took my exit and got into the town, the place was as dry as tinder.

However, I had no difficulty explaining that bad weather had made me late, because I worked at a hospital, and they were in radio contact with the emergency services who reported that it was a near-tornado that had passed through. There had been several motor vehicle accidents, uprooted trees and downed power lines - not a night for someone who is directionally challenged, to be driving!

On another occasion, in the middle of the day, I was driving, on a back road, of course. I suddenly drove into an intense rain shower and everything in front of me turned white! I didn't know where I was or whether I was going forward, reversing or turning. I stepped hard on my brakes, and turned on my hazard lights. Thank God, the driver behind me was going slowly enough to avoid hitting me! He was not pleased!

TRANSFERS

When I lived in Brooklyn, New York, I almost never drove, and as far as I could tell, it seemed like the official position of the powers that be, was to dissuade as many New York City residents as possible from driving, and to persuade us to ride the city buses and trains. I was fine with that, and there were several bus and train routes that could take me to work or home. It was not always a smooth ride, though. Many times, I boarded a bus that was going in the wrong direction. When I discovered my error, I had to go to the front and say, "Driver, I think I'm going in the wrong direction. I need to be going that way (pointing)." Now, interestingly, I was always fascinated by the fact that, on every bus I took, there was at least one person who was riding on a New York City bus for the first time. So, these drivers didn't really make a big deal of passengers being confused. They would stop the bus and allow me to get off. If they were nice, they would give me a transfer and say, "Cross the street, and take the (# -) bus going in the opposite direction." They did that very often, although I didn't often get a transfer.

I also made mistakes while taking the train. Many were the mornings when I left my house in a mad rush - and everybody's in a rush in New York City. You rush either because you're already late, or you don't want to be late. Now here is something that the directionally challenged must bear in mind. If you're on a train, and discover that you're on the wrong train, or the right train, but going in the wrong direction, it is important that you know where to get off that train, because on any given route, there are only so many stations that allow you to change trains, without having to exit the station. There are times when the train line going in one direction is on one side of the street and the line going in the opposite direction is on the other side of the street, so the station is partitioned by the street. If you exit the station, cross the street to enter the station on the other side, you have to pay another fare. I know that from experience. I've had those experiences.

Usually, when the sides of the train station are on either side of the street, only one side will have a ticket-dispensing kiosk. I remember, one day, going down to the kiosk, purchasing my ticket, then crossing, to the other side of the street and entering the station. While I was there, and the train could be seen coming in the distance, I suddenly realized that I was on the wrong side. I panicked, got out and rushed across the street, to try to see if I could catch the train before it left the station. I shouldn't have done that because the very next station that the train on my side would have taken me was one where I could easily have walked across the platform to change trains. However, I was in a hurry, and too discombobulated to think clearly. When I got to the gate of the station, I called out to the ticket agent and asked her to let me in, explaining that I had just bought my ticket from her and had mistakenly entered the station on the wrong side. That nice lady had just seen me, right? I mean, I had bought the ticket from her just a few minutes before. Right? And it was not a crowded station. I was sure that I had been the last person to whom she had sold a ticket, and she could clearly have seen me on the other side of the train track. That woman looked at me from head to toe. She said, "I am not letting you in." Well. I simply stood there until the train came and the disembarking passengers pushed open the gate, then I went in. I *couldn't* pay again!

ATTENTIVENESS

People like us are usually accused, wrongly so, of not paying attention. We do pay attention. But it has to be particular attention, because so many times we confuse places that look alike. If I am not able to read the signs I see on the street; if I'm not looking for differences in the buildings, I'll just not be able to find where I'm going. And like I said, this can happen whether I'm walking or driving. The sad fact is, those who are able to easily find their way misunderstand us and often become impatient with us. For the next chapter, let's consider how the rest of the world sees us and reacts to our vicissitudes.

5
How are the directionally challenged treated?

How do you feel when others realize that you cannot tell your left from your right, or identify the cardinal points? Are you one of those individuals who do their best to disguise this fact, or do you openly admit it? Well, I've never been bashful about the fact that I do not instinctively know my left from my right. And I have been known to argue with others about where east, west, north and south are. I haven't won mmm—any of those arguments!

When I moved to the US, one of my first jobs was as a home health aide. I used to care for an elderly lady in her home. Despite being in her late 90s, this lady was remarkably lucid and cogent, though she suffered from various physical ailments. One of her frequent requests was for me to massage her back. She'd specify, "Up near my shoulder, on my right side." Because I did not instinctively know, I had to stand for a minute or two, trying to determine which side was her right side, and therefore, where I should massage. Since I had a 50-50 chance of being correct when I guessed, I would guess. Many times, I would start massaging, only to hear, "It's the other side." She was not upset, however, but was always very understanding and patient, acknowledging that I had difficulty in distinguishing my left from my right.

She once confided in me, "My daughter is like you." Her daughter possessed an extraordinary singing talent; she was the most gifted singer I had ever encountered. Her voice was so captivating that she could have been the star of any musical or the lead in any opera. Her mother often lamented, "She could have soared to great heights with her singing, but she never learned music. The reason she couldn't learn music was because she couldn't differentiate her right hand from her left hand. I couldn't find a music teacher who was willing to work with her." While I couldn't confirm the truth of what she said, it was a poignant observation shared by this mother.

Reflecting on this young woman's predicament, with the knowledge I now possess, I believe that the issue may have extended beyond a simple inability to differentiate right from left. It's possible that she also had a touch of dyslexia, which may have affected her ability to perceive musical notes as others do. Interestingly, some individuals who struggle with directional challenges also find it difficult to decipher symbols and sequences.

LIKE MOTHER, LIKE DAUGHTER

My daughter was diagnosed with dyslexia when she was about 9 years old. She was both dyslexic and directionally challenged! Here I was, sending my child to one of the most prestigious private schools for pre-high school students in Jamaica, and I was worried out of my mind that she needed expert help but wasn't getting it, despite the school having a program for slow learners.

As a trained teacher, for secondary level students, with some knowledge about how to identify various types of learning disabilities in my students, I assumed that my daughter's early childhood teachers were much more proficient than I was in this area. From the time my child was in Kindergarten, I detected that she was having more than the usual degree of difficulty learning to read. I spoke often with successive teachers and expressed my concerns. Her Kindergarten and Grade One teachers told me not to worry. "Not all children reach reading readiness at the same time," they said. "Just be patient, Mom." I backed off a bit. However, in Grade Two and Grade Three, she still had not started to read. When I suggested that my daughter might have a learning disability, the teachers insisted that was not the case. One even said, "There's nothing wrong with her. She's very intelligent. She can learn. She's just lazy." That same teacher used to send home my daughter's work with this note: "Mrs. Greenland, this is what your daughter wrote in class today. I have no idea what she is trying to say. This appears to me to be written in a foreign language." I am not kidding when I say that I would take that book and read what my daughter had written. Although every word was misspelled and the letters in the words were all jumbled, I understood it perfectly. This was also the case as I would read the work turned in by some of my students who were not the best at penmanship and spelling. Regardless of what they had written, when others could not, I seemed to have a knack for deciphering what they were trying to say. Perhaps, this was a compensatory gift for my not being able to decipher simple navigational directions.

The short ending to the long and painful story of my daughter's reading odyssey, however, is that I had to seek for my child the help she desperately needed. I got her professionally assessed, and yes, she was dyslexic. I enrolled her in an extracurricular program that assisted her in mitigating the effects of this most debilitating challenge. In a little over a year, she had almost caught up with her classmates in reading, but she still struggled with academics. In fact, had we not migrated to the US (where she was instantly placed in a class of "high achievers" - go figure), I believe I would have had to find some vocational occupation for her.

Within a year of being in a US middle school, my daughter made the Dean's Honor Roll, and there has been no stopping her since. Today, she is an accomplished professional who reads well, although she is still a bit afraid of the written word. Because she learned to read at a late age, she developed a preference for auditory prompts, and she still prefers to listen over having to read.

I mention my daughter's experience only because too many individuals who write with their left hand; who cannot distinguish between their right and their left; who are otherwise directionally challenged, or who just function contrary to how "normal" people behave, testify of how their school days were made intolerable by insensitive and ignorant teachers. It turned out that even though I was trained to teach junior high and high school students, and although it was not part of our regular curriculum, my Reading professor (a shout-out to June Diega, wherever she is right now) told us that it would not be unheard-of for a student who "had fallen through the cracks" to arrive in our Grade Seven, Eight, or Nine class, being unable to read.

She explained the signs to look for in identifying a learning disability and provided some remedial steps to take, if such a condition was detected. I had conducted these checks with my daughter and concluded that she did indeed have a problem. However, being emotionally involved, I didn't want to rely solely on my observations. I also assumed that those Kindergarten to Grade Three teachers, who were trained to teach children how to read, actually knew what they were saying, when they told me that my child was not yet reading-ready. Nevertheless, I did not accept the argument that my daughter was lazy, especially since I spent considerable time in the evenings and on weekends helping her with homework that she struggled to complete, witnessing her growing frustration, firsthand.

MISSING THE BUS

When we lived in South Florida, I worked nights, and my husband would drop me off for work at about 6:45 PM and pick me up in the mornings. However, there were times when he was late or couldn't pick me up because of other commitments. On those occasions, I had to walk a certain distance to catch the bus home. Let me tell you, it was always hit or miss when trying to find the bus stop. I would often walk in the wrong direction, as I never did this often enough to familiarize myself with the route.

When I finally reached the street where the bus ran, I would go to the first stop I saw and wait. The wait was always long, as there weren't many buses on that route. I'd see a bus stopping on the other side of the street, but since I didn't know which direction I should be going, I didn't think much of it. When the bus on my side finally arrived, I'd board, pay my fare, and sit down. Only after riding for quite a while would it hit me—I had been standing on the wrong side of the road all along! I had watched the correct bus pass by, and I had ended up taking the bus going in the direction opposite to my destination! This happened multiple times.

By the time I got home, hours later, I would be in a foul mood. My husband would assume I was upset because he hadn't picked me up, and I never bothered to explain that I had likely stayed on the bus until it completed its route and turned around. Getting off sooner wouldn't have helped, as I probably would have had to wait for the same bus to return and pick me up again. Of course, either way meant paying for two fares!

One particularly memorable time, in late fall, the temperature had dropped to around 59°F, which feels like freezing for someone living in Florida. I hadn't dressed warmly the night before, not expecting to be out in the cold the next morning. But there I was, walking to the bus stop in just a thin blouse. I knew which way was north only because of the biting wind that seemed to blow directly from Canada, chilling me to the bone. By the time the bus arrived, I was shivering uncontrollably. But my ordeal wasn't over. The air conditioning on the bus was blasting what felt like arctic temperatures. I approached the driver, but having used public transport in several US cities, I'd had this conversation with drivers before. He said, "The temperature is set at the depot; I can't change it. Eventually, it will be adjusted, but not yet." Amen to that.

So, there I was, having to "chill" for the entire ride—literally. And, to make things worse, I had to endure two bus journeys that day. I chose to stay seated on the bus rather than get off and stand at the bus stop, until probably, that same bus picked me up on its return leg. By the time I got home, I was frosty —in more ways than one.

A MISNOMER

Directional challenge - another name is directional confusion - is often mistakenly referred to as directional dyslexia. This term is a misnomer because being directionally challenged—having difficulty distinguishing cardinal points or left from right—and being dyslexic—struggling to decipher letters and words—are distinct conditions. However, it is possible for one individual to experience both.

I have never been diagnosed with dyslexia, and I consistently performed well in school, often ranking at or near the top of my class. Nevertheless, I do notice that under stress, I tend to confuse symbols, particularly numbers. If I'm stressed and provide you with a number, please double-check it, as it's likely to be mixed up. For instance, if I say "Eight, six, nine," I might have meant to say, "Nine, eight, six."

Also, as a practicing journalist who never learned conventional typing, I primarily type using the fore and middle fingers of both hands while looking at the keyboard. I can type at a speed of 50 to 60 words per minute. This method has served me well, so I never felt the need to learn touch typing. My one drawback is that, sometimes, while looking at the keyboard (not the screen) and spelling out the words as I type, I end up with words in which the order of letters is disrupted. For example, I can be certain that I typed the word "m-o-t-h-e-r," because I was looking at my fingers as I typed. But when I review the document, I may see "o-m-h-t-r-e."

What complicates this issue further is that often it's not the entire word that is rearranged but perhaps, just two letters. It seems there is a glitch in my perception, causing the information about which key is being struck to be incorrect. Then when editing my own work, I often "see" the word spelled correctly, only to realize the error after I have forwarded the document to the intended recipient, and am rereading it. Alarmingly, though rarely, I sometimes interchange the positions of letters or symbols, even when writing by hand!

Despite these challenges, I do not believe I am dyslexic. I can read and make sense of almost any text, even when the words are mixed up or the handwriting is illegible to most people. It turns out, I'm very proficient at reading and identifying errors in others' work, but I struggle to see the errors in my own writing. Additionally, I find it more difficult to edit my work on screen, compared to on paper. Have you ever experienced this?

A COMMON OCCURRENCE

I'm sure you've witnessed a driver sitting at the intersection of a major street and a minor street, possibly hesitating to join the main road due to uncertainty and poor road depth perception. This hesitation can be exacerbated by the stress of other drivers lining up behind, tooting their horns, and making concentration even more difficult. Typically, a bold driver, often a male, will break out of the line, go around the hesitant driver, and dart onto the main road, ignoring the fact that oncoming traffic had to brake suddenly to avoid a collision. This does nothing to boost the confidence of the directionally challenged driver.

Oh, for the days when our difficulties are recognized! Until then, how do we cope with these challenges? This is what we'll explore in the next chapter.

6
How do we handle being directionally challenged?

When did you first realize that you struggled with spatial navigation or couldn't differentiate between your right and left? Was it during your early childhood, your teenage years, or perhaps even later, in adulthood? I've known for as long as I can remember that following navigational directions was almost impossible for me.

SCHOOL STORIES

During my elementary school years, we often participated in physical exercises out on the playing field, involving activities like lifting the right leg or the left arm, and turning to the right or left. These exercises were meant to be fun and engaging. However, I could never quite get them right. I would invariably do the opposite of what was instructed. For instance, if I was told to lift my right arm, I would likely lift my left arm, and I wasn't alone in this struggle; some of my classmates faced the same challenge.

In high school, one of my favorite pastimes was watching the school's cadets during their drill practice sessions. Back then, members of the cadet corps were male students who aspired to join the Jamaica Defense Force as officers after graduating. The US equivalent of the Jamaica Cadet Corps is the Reserve Officers' Training Corps (ROTC). A group of us girls loved to admire these young men in their uniforms, but what truly fascinated us was their precise marching formations.

However, there were moments when even the cadets got confused. I vividly remember them marching along and suddenly receiving different commands, at which point, at least one cadet would turn in the opposite direction—left when they should go right, or right when they should go left. We found it amusing back then, but looking back, I wonder how many of those young men struggled with differentiating their right from their left. At that time, we laughed, whether at ourselves or others, without considering the deeper implications of what it all meant.

THE VILLAGE KLUTZ

Back in the day, my village used to hold community get-to-gethers, with line-dancing in the streets and all sorts of festivities. Without fail, there was always that one person hopelessly out of sync, moving in a direction that was the opposite of everyone else's. That person? Definitely not me. I had no intention of publicly embarrassing myself like that. You see, I've got two left feet, and they're quite heavy. I always said that if anyone wanted to witness me attempting to dance, they'd have to pay for the privilege. There was no chance I was going to pay to become the laughingstock of the village! So, while others might have been going the wrong way in the group dance, rest assured it wasn't me. Although everyone found it amusing at the time, looking back, you can't help but wonder if those poor souls were just directionally challenged.

LONG HAULS

My husband and I used to be frequent road travelers. Although we've slowed down lately, there was a time when we drove up and down the entire Eastern Seaboard of the United States, from Florida to Massachusetts. The biggest issue on these trips? My refusal to help with the driving. It became a point of contention, with his doing all the driving while I sat there feeling guilty, but resolute in my stance. Highways like I-95, I-85, and I-77? No thank you! Every time he'd ask me to drive, I'd respond with a firm, "I can't do that." He'd retort with something like, "You can't do anything." I'd fire back, "There are plenty of things I can do, and do well!" And naturally, he'd challenge that, leading to another phase of the argument, with my listing my strengths and his countering each point I made.

Thankfully, we no longer argue about it. He's come to accept that he enjoys being behind the wheel, and I'm very happy in the passenger seat. Over time, he's also acknowledged that there are indeed many things I can do well—some even better than he can. And note this, my reluctance to drive wasn't because I doubted my driving skills. Rather, it was because of my difficulty in deciphering road signs quickly enough, and my absolute fear of ramps. The idea of accidentally taking the wrong exit, getting lost in an unfamiliar area, and not knowing how to get back on track? That terrifies me to this day. And don't get me started on lane changes.

I always try to stay in the far-right lane, the slow lane, unless I'm avoiding an entrance ramp. But whenever another vehicle merges onto the highway while I'm in the right lane, panic sets in. My depth perception is terrible, and I know it. I can't properly judge if I should continue in the lane and pass the merging vehicle, change lanes in time, or even if I should slow down and let them go ahead—because I'm scared the car behind me might rear-end me! And so, I hesitate, overthink, and often leave my indicator on longer than I should, probably making other drivers wonder what my intentions are.

I constantly question myself about my discomfort while driving. The fact is, I know and observe the road code well. When there are a few vehicles on the highway, I manage just fine. However, heavy traffic unnerves me. Now you know why my GPS chooses back roads for my road trips.

One directionally challenged individual told me, *"I avoid the middle lane like the plague! There are too many people entering and leaving it, either to avoid oncoming traffic from the ramp, or to facilitate overtaking. I prefer the left lane. All I have to do in that lane is keep up with the speed!"*

I am really not comfortable going over the posted speed limit—which is the norm in the leftmost lane, so studiously I avoid that lane. Like I said, I'll try to stay in the right or middle lane. But there's just too much terror involved, whichever lane I'm in!

"I've been affected by this malady all my life. It has cheated me out of a lot of good times and good friends. Whenever I'm with a group and someone suggests that we all meet up somewhere for a drink, I always decline the invite because I'm thinking that it will be hard enough getting home from where I am currently. No use adding a commute to another venue, then having to find my way home from there." - JSP

I remember a time when GPS was not an app on your smart-phone. It was a standalone gadget you'd set up in your vehicle, and it required periodic updates to stay accurate. Without these updates, the directions could be laughably wrong! I recall an incident vividly: I had recently arrived in Fort Lauderdale to visit my son and needed to navigate through unfamiliar territory. Despite getting verbal directions from my son, I decided to use the car's GPS for extra assurance. However, I overlooked one crucial detail—having moved from North Carolina to Florida, I should have updated the GPS. I forgot.

As I drove, I tried to reconcile my son's instructions (which I trusted more) with the GPS directions. At a major intersection, where my son had clearly told me to go straight, the GPS started insisting, "Turn left! Turn left!" Ignoring the GPS, I continued straight. It kept telling me to turn left, and was getting on my last nerve. I wanted to turn it off, but couldn't while driving, so I tried to ignore its nagging.

After a while, the GPS went silent, and I sighed with relief. But as I entered a newly constructed overpass, it suddenly commanded, "Turn right! Turn right!" I shouted back in frustration, "Do you want me to commit suicide? How can I turn right on an overpass?" This bizarre interaction continued for a few minutes. Had someone else been in the car with me, anyone who overheard the din might have thought we were in a heated argument. Instead, I believe passersby just thought I was a raving madwoman. Thankfully, the GPS finally stopped communicating and remained silent for the rest of the journey. However, as I slowly pulled into the driveway of my destination, it chimed in, "You have reached your destination!" I sarcastically retorted, "I did, no thanks to you! If I had listened to you, I would have driven off that bridge."

WE ARE MANY!

So, how widespread do you think this directional confusion is, and how much is known about it? Believe it or not, it's not a well-kept secret. Interestingly, there are communities that offer a sympathetic environment where the directionally challenged from across the globe can share their experiences, commiserate, and provide support to one another. On Facebook, there are some members-only groups. Another support group can be found on The Guardian UK's website, specifically on its Notes and Queries page.

A cursory survey of comments on these platforms confirms that there are striking similarities in the experiences of directionally challenged individuals worldwide. This phenomenon is too significant to go without the global recognition it deserves. Posts on The Guardian's website come from places as diverse as Australia, Canada, England, Germany, India, Ireland, Malaysia, New Zealand, Oman, Scotland, Singapore, South Africa, Taiwan, Uganda, and the United States.

New members to the support groups for the directionally challenged often express immense relief, revealing that they had spent their entire lives thinking they were the only ones experiencing such confusion. Recurring themes include frequently getting lost, being misunderstood and mischaracterized, feelings of frustration and shame, and a deep desire for recognition. Whether you call it directional challenge/confusion, directional disorientation, developmental topographical disorientation, directional dyslexia, spatial or geographic dyslexia—it's undeniably a global issue.

"I spent large chunks of my time getting lost; until GPS changed my life." - Loz K

PROVIDENTIAL CARE

There are moments when I feel uncertain about my actions on the road, and I must acknowledge that it's solely by God's mercy that I have avoided any accidents. Despite having a flawless driving record, and being a fairly competent driver, it is divine protection that keeps me safe. I must emphasize this fact. Before every journey, I pray fervently. During the trip, I continue praying fervently. The entire time I'm behind the steering wheel, I am in constant prayer, asking the Lord to guide me safely to my destination and back. After each trip, I express my profound gratitude to Him. I often say that He is my pilot, and that's the truth, because I truly cannot drive without His guidance. Incidentally, my daughter tells me that she also prays before driving; continuously while driving, and after she gets to her destination.

Now, I strongly recommend that all drivers pray for divine guidance before embarking on any journey, especially on increasingly hazardous roads. However, there is a special group, including you and me, that must pray every moment we're behind the wheel, because we face these daunting experiences and challenges. And we must also pray for greater global understanding of our situation.

SO, WHAT'S THE VERDICT?

Many of the experiences I've related are my own, but I know you have had similar ones. Indeed, contributors to the various platforms that welcome comments from the directionally challenged testify to the shared reality of our group—the total angst we feel. Recurring themes of concern include frequently getting lost, even in small buildings or familiar areas, being misunderstood and mischaracterized, frustration and shame, and the deep desire for recognition of our struggles. Having explored these personal experiences related to being direction-ally challenged, we will want to validate them by discussing some scientific explanations. In the next chapter, we will endeavor to better understand our condition as we further explore how it manifests.

7

What role does our brain play in our lostness?

Have you ever truly *been* lost? I ask that question because there is a difference between *feeling* lost and *being* lost. For those of us who struggle with navigation, moving from one place to another can often be a source of confusion. Many times, we feel lost even when we're in familiar surroundings. For example, if you ask me to point to a location I know well, chances are I'll point in the wrong direction! So, I'd feel lost, not knowing which direction to take; and, I've gotten lost in various villages, towns, and cities. But in reality, I wasn't lost. There were always people milling around, so I could have asked for directions, and many times, I did.

Being lost, on the other hand, is a different ballgame. This is the substance of which nightmares are made! It is a situation from which even navigationally savvy individuals might not escape, and the directionally challenged have next to no chance of surviving. It's one of those times when we think, "This place not only looks unfamiliar; it is unfamiliar!" Or, "I've never been here, don't know how I got here, and don't know how to get back!" Has that ever happened to you?

When we're navigating familiar areas that suddenly appear unfamiliar, that feeling can create a sense of unease and confusion. But there's still a small voice in the back of our minds reminding us, "I'm supposed to know where I am." However, in truly unfamiliar areas, that confusion can escalate into fear and panic, undermining any attempt to reorient ourselves. We end up moving in a heightened state of anxiety, and this confusion can manifest in many ways.

Thank God, I don't think I was ever truly lost, but the fact is, *feeling* lost is scary enough! What do you think?

HERE'S WHAT SOME EXPERTS SAY

In his 2020 book *From Here to There*, Michael Bond discusses "the psychology of lostness." He explains that stress and anxiety disrupt the cognitive functions essential to navigation (p.168). Since humans are creatures of habit, most of us—even those with a good sense of direction—prefer to stay within familiar or at least similar environments. Unfortunately, those of us who are directionally challenged don't have that luxury; even familiar places can seem strange.

The late Dr. Roger Sperry, a renowned neuropsychologist, neurobiologist, and cognitive neuroscientist, discovered that left-brain-dominant individuals often process information analytically, breaking it down into smaller pieces and examining each one separately. In contrast, he says, right-brain-dominant individuals tend to approach information holistically, using pattern recognition to solve problems. I propose that there is a third group—those who frequently use both analysis and synthesis. I consider myself part of that group. While I don't always switch between these modes seamlessly, I often find that I can both appreciate the forest and examine each tree simultaneously. Do you know anyone who identifies with this approach?

In a study by Ehet et al. (2006), the left hemisphere was shown to be particularly effective in forming associations in memory, selective attention, and positive emotions, in addition to controlling right-hand dominance. The right hemisphere, while controlling the left side of the body, was found to be involved in pitch perception, arousal, and negative emotions. However, the researchers cautioned that many studies have produced inconsistent results regarding which, if any one hemisphere is solely responsible for certain functions. They suggest that it might be more accurate to attribute these abilities to the *interaction* between the hemispheres, facilitated by the corpus callosum, the network of nerve fibers connecting both sides of the brain.

Tansan, Nguyen, and Newcombe (2022) point out that successful navigation relies on several abilities. One is gauging the distance between objects and their directions relative to each other. Another is recognizing permanent landmarks and using them to create mental maps. For people like me, these tasks can be difficult. Retracing steps is also a challenge. I find that on the return leg of a journey, I'll often notice a completely new set of landmarks, and the ones I remember may seem entirely different! It's not uncommon for me to travel a familiar route and suddenly notice a building or landmark that seems brand new. The question is, did I never notice it before, or did I see it but failed to remember it?

"I tell people I can usually find my way to their house, without GPS, if I've been there about 100 times, and even then, only if I'm really concentrating. Initially, of course, they'll laugh at what they think is an exaggeration, and then they find out it isn't. I've

had people say, 'Oh yes. I'm bad with directions, too.' But they just don't get it. For me, it's more than that. It's visiting my son's family, once a week, for years. His house is only 20 minutes away from where I live, and I will get lost on the way home, every time that my GPS doesn't work. By the time I manage to find my way home, I'm crying and shaking." - K.C.

SPATIAL NAVIGATION

Spatial cognition and navigational ability encompass a wide range of specific skills. These include identifying points in space, determining the orientation of lines and objects, assessing location in depth, understanding geometric relationships between objects, and processing motion, including motion in depth. Notably, these spatial skills can be applied to both imagined and external objects. Personally, I seem to have a deficit in all these functions.

David Uttal, a cognitive scientist at Northwestern University, has long struggled with directional challenges. He has also done extensive studies on spatial cognition. Recalling a significant incident from his youth, he shares, "When I was 13 years old, I got lost on a Boy Scout hike, and I was lost for two and a half days." Uttal admits that he still faces difficulties in navigating his surroundings (Holmes, 2024).

David Uttal's experience mirrors that of many individuals who frequently lose their way, even in familiar settings. Like Uttal, I have always had a propensity for getting lost, and I suspect that you might have experienced this as well. Often, my challenge lies in recognizing the same landmarks that I pass daily. This difficulty is only magnified when encountering entirely new landmarks. Interestingly, many of us perform well in locating objects and places on paper, such as on a map. Consider the diagram below, for example.

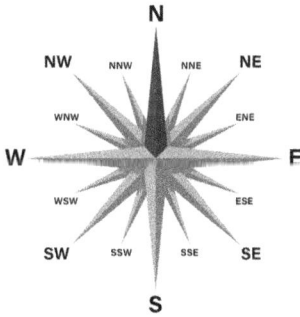

In this representation of a Google Map, making the actual trip from Madison Street to ACME Markets and back would require memorizing two entirely different sets of landmarks. However, by simply looking at the map, I can easily determine that Travolo di Palmisano is somewhat north-northeast of ACME Markets, while Grand Vin lies south-southwest of Otto Strada. In other words, I can make pronouncements about these locations and discuss them intelligently only because I'm viewing them on paper. For me to navigate to these places, in real life, would be a different story. A simple one-way trip might be manageable, but navigating to multiple locations, especially with factors like traffic signals, road conditions, construction, or even the weather? That becomes much more complex. How would you handle it?

According to Tansan, Nguyen, and Newcombe (2022), the ability of the directionally challenged to recognize a place from a specific viewpoint is limited. This impairment, as the researchers explain, arises from difficulty in combining external environmental cues, such as permanent landmarks, with internal cues stored in memory. From my point of view, how much I've retained and can access depends largely on the proper functioning of my vestibular, proprioceptive, and motor systems.

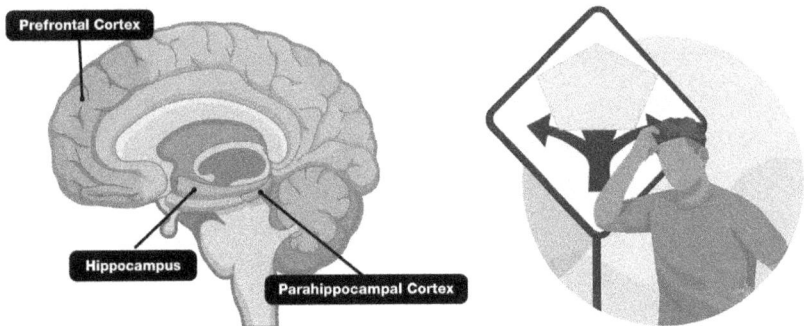

The vestibular system, primarily consisting of the semicircular canals and the otoliths, is crucial for detecting the head's orientation, and acceleration in any direction. It enables necessary compensations in eye movement and body posture. Working in concert with the cochlea in the inner ear, and the visual system, the vestibular system informs our sense of balance and spatial orientation, coordinating movement with equilibrium. The proprioceptive system also plays a vital role. It includes neurosensory receptors distributed throughout our nervous system, and particularly in the motor system – the muscles, joints, and tendons. The hippocampus interacts with both the vestibular and motor systems to aid in spatial orientation and navigation from one location to another. Constant messaging from neurosensory receptors to the brain about our positions and actions ensures that, under normal circumstances, we are aware of our location and can execute appropriate movements.

However, if the collaboration between these systems falters, disorientation ensues. If the vestibular and visual systems provide conflicting information, for example, the vestibular system detects movement while the visual system perceives a stationary position—motion sickness can occur. This phenomenon is common among those who are directionally challenged. Personally, I find that my sitting in a swing chair induces immediate motion sickness. The circular motion of the swing chair gives me the impression of movement, while my eyes report that I'm simply sitting. This seems to trigger nausea and vertigo-like symptoms. Additionally, I suspect that my fear of heights and the unease I feel when looking down from high places may be linked to a malfunctioning vestibular system. Have you experienced similar sensations?

WHAT GOES INTO SPATIAL NAVIGATION?

Ensuring our body is properly oriented or positioned while traveling is crucial. Consider the complexity of the process: numerous sensors, receptors, and neurons collaborate to allow us to simply stand or sit, and face a certain direction. It's remarkable to realize the intricate coordination required just to move from point A to point B. We must be oriented to our starting point, current location, and destination. Not everyone naturally has this capability.

Reflecting on my childhood travels, I now understand that my perception of vehicular movement as circular stemmed from a misaligned proprioception or kinesthesia. The lack of coordination between my vestibular and visual systems caused me to develop motion sickness. To alleviate the dizziness, I would close my eyes while the vehicle was in motion, which meant I couldn't see where I was going. Even with my eyes open, the circular perception prevented me from recognizing the route. I couldn't memorize landmarks and, despite feeling the vehicle turn, I couldn't determine the direction. Sometimes, even after the vehicle stopped, and with my eyes still closed, I still perceived motion. This disconnect between external cues and my underdeveloped internal mental maps hindered my ability to navigate effectively.

I now believe that despite noting landmarks during travel, my vestibular, proprioceptive, and motor systems do not provide the appropriate internal cues for proper navigation. This insight sheds light on my ongoing challenges with spatial orientation and directional sense.

While we need more in-depth studies in this field, it is clear that the role of each hemisphere is not easily observed in the day-to-day activities of a healthy person. Yet, studies on brain activity in individuals with conditions such as epilepsy or stroke support the theory that the hemispheres have specialized functions. In severe cases of epilepsy, when doctors sever the corpus callosum to stop seizures, or when a stroke renders this connection ineffective, the hemispheres can become disjointed. Studies show that damage to one hemisphere often results in paralysis on the opposite side of the body.

Another important discovery, once thought impossible, is that new brain cells can be produced throughout a person's life. This was observed in studies of London cab drivers, as will be mentioned in Chapter 8. More significantly, it appears that functions traditionally associated with one hemisphere can still be performed even after that hemisphere has been damaged or removed.

One incident that has demonstrated the versatility of the hemispheres, and, to me, raised even more questions, concerned the experience of a little girl named Jody Miller. Previously, the scientific community had believed a complete brain with both hemispheres intact was absolutely necessary for someone to live a normal life. This popular belief was challenged by the case of Jody, who suffered from a rare condition called Rasmussen's Encephalitis. This condition caused her to have frequent life-threatening seizures originating from the right side of her brain, and leading to severe paralysis on the left side of her body. When every known treatment had failed to cure Jody, the only choice her doctors had was hemispherectomy, a procedure in which half of the brain is surgically removed. Although unsure about the success of the procedure, surgeons went ahead and removed the right half of Jody's brain in an attempt to alleviate her seizures.

To their surprise, the surgery was successful. Jody's seizures ceased, and she recovered from the surgery incredibly well. Immediately following the surgery, she had slight paralysis, on the left side of the body, which was later treated with physiotherapy. According to the doctors, her left hemisphere was able to take over the role of the missing right hemisphere. This phenomenon is known as neuroplasticity: the brain being capable of rewiring and modifying its connections, to restore a lost function. Jody was able to graduate college, win multiple scholarships and awards, and live a normal, healthy life — all with only half a brain! – *Inkspire, 2018*

While this case is extraordinary, a study from the University of Utah found that, in most cases, both hemispheres collaborate to perform cognitive tasks. This study supports the notion that many people utilize both hemispheres for most activities. I am particularly intrigued by this research and plan to explore it further in a later chapter.

Finally, the research findings I have uncovered make me more aware of how the crucial collaboration between my vestibular, proprioceptive, and motor systems sometimes fail, leading to improper spatial orientation and navigation. However, I have to recognize that scientists have made substantial progress in advancing our understanding of the brain functions related to spatial memory and navigation. In the next chapter, we'll continue to explore what experts are uncovering about our challenges with navigation.

8
What has science discovered?

How are individuals who are directionally challenged perceived by some in the scientific community? According to Dr. Benton St Cyr, a psychologist and psychotherapist, those who struggle with directional awareness might excel in various tasks unrelated to spatial orientation. Dr. St Cyr labels these individuals as "spatially or geographically dyslexic." While I hesitate to identify as dyslexic because I do not have difficulties with words, I do experience challenges with directions and orientation. Therefore, a term like "dysorientia" might better describe my condition. This is a concept I considered after visiting the website: https://www.dyslexia-reading-well.com/. It is worth noting that some people with dyslexia may also struggle with orientation, highlighting similar difficulties, such as the inability to memorize and follow directions.

Dr. Eleanor Maguire, formerly a Professor of Cognitive Neuroscience at University College London's School of Life & Medical Sciences, dedicated much of her career to studying spatial abilities. She is renowned for her work with London cab drivers, who had to undergo an intense two-year training program that involved navigating approximately 25,000 streets and identifying around 20,000 landmarks in the city. The complexity of these streets has been likened to "a tangle of yarn that a preschooler glued on construction paper" (Jabr, 2011). Before earning their taxi licenses, these drivers were rigorously tested on their knowledge of the area. Dr. Maguire's research assessed these drivers at the beginning of their training and again four years later.

Using Magnetic Resonance Imaging (MRI), the study revealed that cab drivers who successfully completed the training and worked for over two years, exhibited significant growth in their hippocampal region of the brain. Specifically, they had more brain matter in one part of the hippocampus than they did at the start of their training. Their hippocampi were also larger than those of unsuccessful applicants and individuals in the control group.

Interestingly, the research found that while the posterior region of the hippocampus grew, aiding the drivers in recalling or planning complex routes, the anterior portion of the hippo-campus shrank. This anterior shrinkage correlated with poorer performance on visual memory tests, indicating a trade-off in brain functions.

The study by Dr. Maguire also found that the London taxi drivers' hippocampi reverted to their original sizes once the cab drivers retired or changed to jobs that did not require the storage of large amounts of spatial data. I'm not sure if the visual memory of these former cab drivers improved, or if their anterior hippocampi regrew, as their posterior hippocampi regained their former sizes. The interesting fact is that it's not just any data, but spatial data that will stretch the posterior hippocampus. The posterior hippocampi of medical doctors and persons who received special memory training showed no increase despite the expanse of the data their hippocampi had to store.

While at Boston University, neurologist, Howard Eichenbaum was quoted as saying, "[I]t really was the training process that caused the growth in the brain. It shows that you can produce profound changes in the brain with training. That's a big deal" (Jabr, 2011). Howard Eichenbaum was also a leading scholar in the study of the hippocampus.

MORE QUESTIONS THAN ANSWERS

One interesting factor to be considered about Dr. Maguire's study is that the researchers only tested right-handed males, between the ages of 32 and 62. If the results could be applied to other cohorts, could it be presumed that at least some individuals who have difficulty with navigation may actually possess smaller than normal posterior hippocampi? Could it also be true, that, as happened with the London cab drivers, the posterior hippocampus can be stimulated to grow, allowing for an increase in the spatial navigational ability of an individual?

We also have to ask this question: If the hippocampus, which is so crucial to proper navigation, can in fact increase in size, could it be that many persons who are directionally challenged, by giving up on their efforts to navigate, are doing themselves a disservice? While only an MRI can show whether or not there is growth in the hippocampus, as a result of our making concerted effort to navigate between locations, isn't it conceivable that if we just keep trying, even if we don't always succeed, we could reduce our stress levels, as we repeatedly endeavor to navigate? This is certainly an area in which Dr. Maguire's work should be continued. There should also be studies to ascertain if other types of activities can foster growth in the posterior hippocampus.

Visual Reorientation Illusions (VRIs) and Developmental Topographical Disorientation (DTD)

There is a group that delves into the perplexing phenomenon known as visual reorientation illusions (VRIs), which explains why we sometimes experience navigational confusion. This intriguing phenomenon is also currently under investigation by the Donders Institute for Brain, Cognition and Behavior, in Nijmegen, the Netherlands, among other research centers. The term VRI originated from observations of astronauts in space, where zero gravity can cause their feet to be where their head should be. Interestingly, astronauts do not experience VRIs on Earth; these illusions are exclusive to the zero-gravity environment, affecting their perception of up and down directions.

However, on Earth, directionally challenged individuals can struggle to navigate from point A to point B, not because they feel their feet are where their head should be, but due to a different kind of VRI. According to Hugh Reid, a proponent of VRI, our bearings can get turned around, causing us to perceive north, south, east, and west in different positions. Reid explains that when we first notice our familiar surroundings becoming unfamiliar, it indicates a non-normal orientation of our location. This disoriented state can persist for an indeterminate period until our brain "suddenly does a VRI flip," and everything quickly returns to its normal orientation. This phenomenon could explain why many individuals who get lost, and sometimes tragically die, are often found extremely close to major road ways or centers of civilization. One conclusion has to be that they were experiencing VRIs, and therefore, were unable to navigate to those locations.

I came across the data on this phenomenon only recently, but I have been experiencing it all my life. I believe VRI explains why, as a young child traveling in a motor vehicle, I saw the trees and buildings appearing to move in a circular direction and assuming various positions and angles. Even today, this experience extends further when I travel by airplane. Sitting by the window, although I'm by no means, in zero gravity, I often get the distinct sensation of flying upside down, especially when the sky and ocean both appear blue above and below the plane. Despite knowing I am not upside down, my perception tells me otherwise, demonstrating a VRI concerned with up and down directions.

Reid suggests that some level of VRI can happen to most people, whether or not they are directionally challenged. For those who are directionally challenged, this can be bewildering as the locations of streets and buildings appear displaced. I have experienced being turned around after exiting the subway or even after leaving a room in a large building.

Reid, who has experienced VRIs since childhood, claims he has honed his ability to reorient his visualizations at will and even enjoys doing so. I, on the other hand, find no humor or pleasure in the disorientation. For example, my husband and I were traveling on a very familiar stretch of road in our town, where we had been living for almost five years. He was driving, of course. We were heading to our church. Suddenly, he made what I thought was a turn to take us back home. I was concerned, but I didn't say anything. A few minutes later, he made another "wrong" turn, and to me, it now appeared that we were going in a circle. I had to ask, "Why did you turn there? Where are we going?" I was concerned that if we didn't stick to the regular route, we were going to be late for Church! My husband said, "Be quiet. This is the way we drive to Church every week." It certainly did not seem that way to me. Even though I had some idea of the general vicinity in which we were, the place appeared totally strange. It certainly did not look like the way we traveled every week. To avoid an argument, I kept quiet, but we had to travel another mile or so, before the place gradually became familiar to me again, and I had to admit that it was in fact our regular route.

There was nothing voluntary about that VRI, if indeed it was a VRI, and I did not enjoy the experience. In fact, I was grateful that I was not the driver, because I would have panicked, stopped and turned around, adding even more time and confusion to my trip. As I said, I've had this experience before. I just didn't know that there was a name for it. In fact, VRIs explain a good deal of my traveling experiences. This is another area in which a great deal of study is imperative.

Even for the spatially oriented, VRIs occur in seemingly straightforward situations such as when they exit the subway or a movie theater. The unreality of the theater atmosphere and the movie, as well as the underground environment, can blur the lines between imagination and reality, causing disorientation until the brain "turns the world around" back to normal.

If any of this sounds familiar to you, consider exploring the Visual Reorientation Illusions (VRIs) group, led by Hugh Reid. Information can be found on their Facebook page at *https://www.facebook.com/groups/1641368339467014/.* More information can be also be found at *https://www.quora.com/ Why-do-we-feel-disoriented-for-a-few-minutes-after-watching- a-movie-in-a-theater and https://blog.donders.ru.nl/?p=14135& lang=en.*

DEVELOPMENTAL TOPOGRAPHICAL DISORIENTATION (DTD)

Some individuals who struggle with navigation may have developmental topographical disorientation (DTD). This means they never developed the ability to create mental images (cognitive constructs or maps) of their surroundings. Therefore, whether they are in a familiar or unfamiliar place, they are unable to orient themselves or navigate from one point to another. They cannot rely on internal mental images to recall where they have been or what they've seen. DTD is more severe than conditions like visual reorientation illusions (VRI), where a person can generate mental images, but struggles to make sense of them. Individuals with DTD cannot form any mental images of their environment—they rely solely on what they can see in the moment.

Here's an example of someone who experiences VRIs:

"I once heard someone say they always go the extra mile, not because they are extra accommodating, but because they missed their exit. For me, it's not just the extra mile; it's the extra miles, because it takes me a long time to even realize I've missed the exit.

I've been dealing with VRIs all my life. While driving through familiar areas, I can suddenly lose all sense of where I am, even though I've traveled the route hundreds of times. I have a mental map of where I started and where I'm supposed to go, but it becomes useless in these moments. When I find myself lost, I have three options. If it's safe, I pull over and try to reorient myself. If that doesn't work, I turn around and drive to a familiar spot to start over. Sometimes, I just keep driving, hoping something will eventually look familiar or that I'll find a safe place to stop. Most of the time, this means driving extra miles and wasting more time, all while my stress levels are on the rise. Of course, there are some days when I manage to make the trip without a problem." – KMN

Now, compare that to someone living with DTD:

I live in Winnipeg, Manitoba, and the building where I work as an office manager is about 2 km (a mile) from my home. Despite the distance being relatively short, my daily commute is traumatic. Even though I pass the same landmarks—like a well-known coffee shop—twice a day, they seem brand new to me each time. It doesn't matter how often I've seen them; I have no recollection of having seen them before on that route; there's no recognition.

I also get lost in my office building. Every time I visit the restroom [near] the end of our hallway, when I make my exit, I don't know if my office is to the right or to the left. I have to ask for directions to find my way back to my office. Because this is so embarrassing, I try my best to avoid using the ladies' room at work. I will go only if it's an absolute necessity.

Traveling to and from work is bad enough. Traveling to a new place completely fills me with dread, and even routine trips totally overwhelm me. Every time, I back my car out of my driveway, even if I'm going to the store, I know, in terms of having an address, where I'm supposed to go, but I don't know how to get there! I can't remember what the store looks like. And it doesn't matter how many times I've been there before! I have to rely either on my GPS, or written directions, to just know which way to turn. My anxiety over getting lost is constant. My biggest fear is having my phone battery die while I'm driving, or entering a dead zone, which has happened more than once.

What others may regard as simple tasks—traveling to work, going to the grocery store, visiting a friend—are extremely daunting to me. Consequently, I've curtailed my travels to only what is

absolutely necessary. I therefore avoid outings and social activities and I even refuse to pursue any new job opportunities. I know both my career and social life are suffering, but it's all I can do at the moment. – JL

Thankfully, I have a healthy imagination, and can generate all the mental images I want. If I could get them into a proper working order, my directional challenges would all be overcome. I get lost easily, even in places I've visited several times. My way of getting around, and of giving others directions, is to point out landmarks - a big billboard, a building with a green roof, a fountain, etc. I avoid new and strange places, and stick to the well beaten paths, even though, in a flash, any of those well-beaten paths can appear absolutely new to me. Accompanying this sense of disorientation is a profound anxiety; a palpable unease stemming from the inability to navigate the world as effortlessly as others seem to do.

How do you rate yourself, regarding VRIs and DTD? Chances are, you may have experienced one of these forms of directional confusion at some point or the other.

Interestingly, according to Hugh Reid, some individuals can be affected by both conditions simultaneously! What's particularly intriguing is that experts unanimously agree that people with Developmental Topographical Disorientation (DTD) may exhibit no signs of brain injury or any degenerative brain diseases. These individuals typically seem to have normal memory, attention, and other cognitive functions. It is specifically in the realm of spatial cognition that they seem to encounter difficulties. Individuals with DTD may exhibit symptoms related to directional confusion, from a very young age, though they might not receive a proper diagnosis until adulthood. One reason for the delayed diagnosis is the striking similarity between the symptoms of DTD and those of other forms of directional confusion.

> *"I have absolutely no idea how people effortlessly point in the direction something is located without being able to see it. How do people know where the front gate/elevator/classroom/parking lot, etc. is located, when you can't see it?"* – LDS

Our lives are not easy, but despite challenges such as our inability to properly navigate, we are still highly capable in other areas! A positive spin on our situation is that we'll never be bored, because every moment, we'll have the opportunity to look at familiar things as if we're seeing them for the first time!

But there's more to explore. Does being right- or left-handed affect our navigational abilities? Also, apart from the typical left- and right-handedness, or the rare ambidexterity, are there other ways handedness is manifested, or may play a role in how we navigate? Although much research remains to be done, in the next chapter, we'll further explore what we already know about this intriguing subject.

9

Center-Brained: Why you can't tell your left from your right

Have you ever found yourself lost in thought while walking, only to suddenly refocus and realize you're on a direct collision course with another person coming from the opposite direction? Then, did it seem that both of you had been equally absorbed in your own worlds, prompting that awkward dance of sidestepping until one of you decides to pause and let the other pass? This scenario unfolds all too frequently for me, and it might be connected to my ongoing struggle with directional confusion. But what about signs, particularly those ubiquitous road signs we encounter daily? Do you feel they're never optimally placed on the roadways? Do you believe they should be directly in your line of sight rather than off to the side? It often feels as though my brain struggles to process signs that are oriented to the right or left.

My long-held opinion, not just through personal observation, but also from undergoing various tests, is that I'm neither left- nor right-handed. Also, the conclusion that I am significantly directionally challenged has been confirmed over the past sixty years, based on my experiences. I also believe that if I had been allowed the freedom to use both hands as I wished, I might have developed a notable level of ambidexterity. Currently, I can switch hands for most tasks, although some actions are more proficiently performed with one hand than with the other. For instance, I throw and bowl with my left hand, but when it comes to batting, my right hand takes the lead. Based on my research, these tendencies suggest that neither the left nor the right hemisphere of my brain is dominant.

It is indeed true, that there are individuals who were right-brained and left-handed, as well as left-brained and right-handed, who currently face challenges with spatial cognition. Some of these individuals might have experienced a disruption in their natural hand preference due to adverse circumstances, some of which we'll explore later. These adverse circumstances potentially cause confusion or a change in people's hand dominance. Consequently, they may now be both left-brained and left-handed, or both right-brained and right-handed, and still struggle with directional challenges. This is not to ignore the fact that there are individuals who are distinctly right-handed or left-handed without any history of trauma or external influence forcing a change in hand dominance, yet they still acknowledge difficulties with directions.

Furthermore, there exist individuals who do not exhibit a clear dominance of either the right or left brain, yet they, too, experience significant challenges with directions. I can attest to this, personally, as I am one such individual, and I have encountered many others who share my predicament. This group of people is often compelled to follow instructions designed for those who are either right-handed or left-handed—predominantly right-handed—and we encounter considerable difficulty adhering to these guidelines!

So, is there another dimension of handedness that has escaped the notice of experts? While we can classify individuals as right-hand-dominant, left-hand-dominant, or even ambidextrous, how do we categorize the multitude of people who do not fit into these established categories? I present myself as Exhibit A. I am neither left-handed nor right-handed, nor am I ambidextrous. Therefore, I propose a new categorization summed up in the following:

The adage "Two is company, three is a crowd" might suggest that the number three complicates matters, yet the number three is profoundly embedded in nature and in human experiences. Our brains seem to have an intrinsic affinity for the number three, as evidenced by the numerous ways we organize our world around this number. When verbalizing, we often group numbers in threes, such as 743, 526, 110, without even consciously realizing it. This could be because the number three is the smallest number needed to create a pattern, which our brains are particularly adept at recognizing and processing.

Three-pronged groupings are prevalent in everyday language and activities. In races, the starting commands are "On your marks, Set, Go!" In education, the basics are often summarized as Reading, Writing, and Arithmetic. Hard work is famously described as requiring blood, sweat, and tears. When we learn the alphabet, we say we know our a-b-c, and we regard something simple, as, easy as 1-2-3. Even our day is divided into morning, noon, and night, while for locations, we say here, there and everywhere. Our meals are labeled as breakfast, lunch, and dinner, and musical scales begin with doh, re, mi. This pattern of threes extends across many facets of life.

Could our brain's functionality also reflect this rule of three? While traditional science identifies only two brain hemispheres, the right and the left, could there be a third dimension or area within the brain that influences our cognition and behavior? Is it conceivable that a central brain region, perhaps involving the corpus callosum that connects them, and the two hemispheres, could form a tripartite structure? Although this central "sphere" might allow one of the three areas to become dominant at different times, depending on the task or situation, each of these three areas would need to work in harmony to ensure the effective orientation and functioning of the individual. This is necessary, as no single hemisphere can be solely responsible for all cognitive processes.

The degree to which these brain areas can operate independently or collaboratively could affect our ability to navigate and understand the world around us. This triadic concept might offer new insights into how we process information and adapt to our environment, suggesting that the rule of three is as vital internally as it is externally.

Even in the absence of a concrete physiological structure, there may exist a conceptual third dimension to the brain. Intellectually, it is plausible that we transcend the simple dichotomy of being either left-brained or right-brained. Many individuals, myself included, find themselves in a state of uncertainty. We can't firmly identify as ambidextrous, and are confused about whether we are inherently left-handed or right-handed. Some of us can attest that during our formative years, we *were* subject to some influence that discouraged the use of our left hand.

Could it be that when one begins to lean towards the dominant use of one side, an interruption in this process results in neither right nor left brain dominance, leaving us in a sort of cognitive limbo? If this is the case, might our ambivalence regarding hand dominance correlate with our struggle to distinguish left from right?

I am inclined to think so. If this is true, how does the ambiguity influence our ability to orient ourselves with the four cardinal directions in the real world? Moreover, is it too speculative to suggest that while the right hemisphere may govern certain functions and the left hemisphere others, the central region—potentially including parts of both hemispheres and the corpus callosum—might also assert dominance in specific tasks? If this hypothesis holds, it explains why my brain fails to identify a dominant hand. I am, in essence, a being governed by a tripartite collective, and there are many others like me. As a center-brained individual, I lack a dominant side.

There is a pressing need for further research to explore this phenomenon.

Could it be that there are three distinct regions of the brain governing our cognitive functions, instead of two?

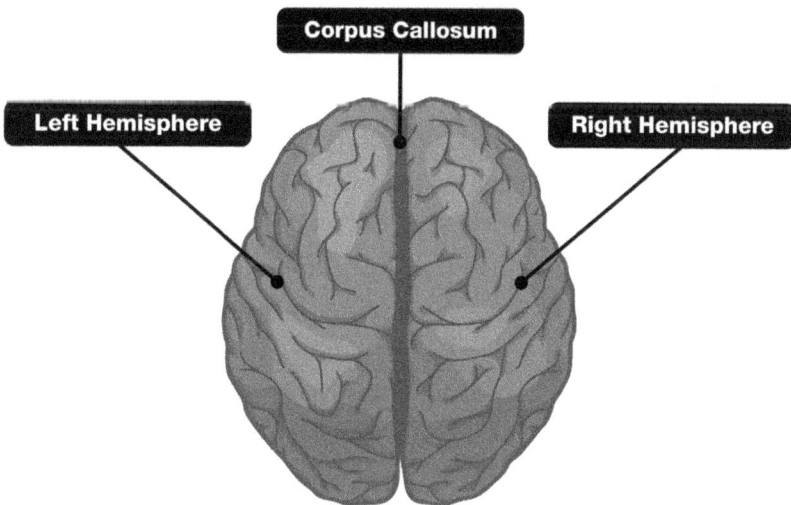

Corpus Callosum

Left Hemisphere

Right Hemisphere

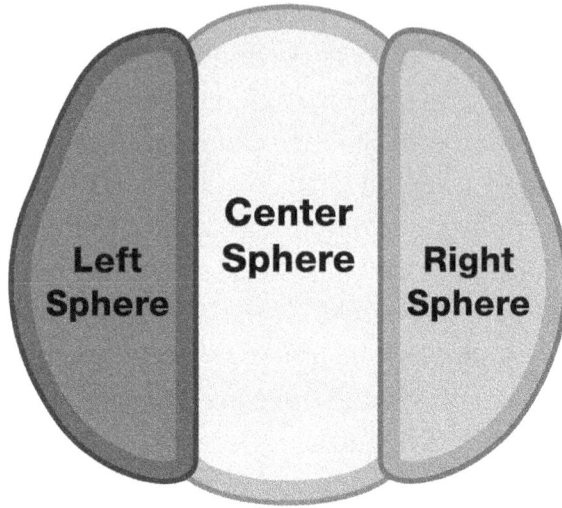

Three Brain Regions

The notion of being "center-brained" suggests a harmonious blend of both left-brained and right-brained traits, allowing an individual to adeptly access both analytical and creative thinking processes. While the left-brain/right-brain dominance theory is well-known, some experts argue that it oversimplifies the complexity of brain functions. My interpretation of this view is that there is much more to unravel about the human brain. Experts posit that both hemispheres are actively engaged in nearly all cognitive activities and that substantial interaction occurs between the two. I believe the key lies within this "interaction."

I propose that individuals who consistently employ a fusion of right and left hemisphere functions are center-brained. I identify as center-brained, because I'm neither right-handed or left-handed. Although I toss a ball with my left hand, I'm not really left-handed. I write with my right hand, but I am not strictly right-handed. I was strongly encouraged to use my right hand to write, but I believe I could have just as easily written with my left hand. I can kick a football with either foot, but I feel my right leg is stronger. My left eye and ear are dominant, yet both sides of my body share tasks and collaborate effectively. When washing dishes, the sponge and dish can be in either hand without issue. If I'm toting something heavy, I can effortlessly switch hands. I attribute this to being center-brained. I believe that because I'm center-brained, when I exit a room, or when I enter an intersection, and I know I should turn left, there is nothing in my head telling me which direction is left.

Previously, I noted that right-handed individuals, when instructed to turn or locate something to their right or left, often engage in internal dialogues to determine direction. For those like me, if the brain signals, "It's to your dominant/weaker side," the body responds, "I have no dominant/weaker side!" People like me take considerable time consulting an internal formula to discern their right from their left, a process made more challenging if they also experience memory issues.

We are finding out that there are so many variations of hand and side dominance, that merely being right-brain or left-brain dominant cannot fully explain all the variations. We need to know much more about how these factors can influence one's ability to self-situate and to navigate.

CENTER-BRAINED EXPLAINED

The term "center-brained" is not an established concept in neuroscience or psychology. Traditional discussions about brain function often reference being "left-brained" or "right-brained." However, the center-brained individual is a fascinating specimen. Unlike our left-brained or right-brained counterparts, center-brained individuals do not rely heavily on either hemisphere of the brain. Instead, we utilize a balanced approach, drawing on both hemispheres more or less equally, to navigate the world around us. This unique cognitive style can lead to some interesting challenges, particularly when it comes to spatial orientation, and moving from Point A to Point B.

For most people, this is a relatively straightforward task. But for the center-brained individual, it can be a bit more complicated since we do not rely on one hemisphere of the brain more than the other, to help us decipher direction. And while we're told that a right-brain-dominant person is more creative, intuitive, imaginative, and better at spatial awareness, and the left-brain-dominant person is more logical, analytical, accurate, and competent with languages, there are millions of us - center-brained individuals - who are a combination of those qualities! In fact, where these functions are concerned, we may be jack of all trades, but master of none. I, for example, could be left-brain-dominant, but for the fact that I'm clueless where spatial awareness is concerned! I believe that I'm logical (although that could be a fallacy) and I try to be analytical. My accuracy is nothing to write home about, especially when my quirks with writing or typing are considered.

There remain numerous questions for which we continue to seek answers. Upon delving further into scientific perspectives on the brain, I discovered that, although I independently conceived of the idea of a third dimension to the brain's hemispheres, I am not alone in this thought. Others have also ventured down this intellectual path!

One such individual was the late Professor Michael Corballis, a distinguished figure in the field of cognitive neuroscience. He dedicated much of his career to studying the intricacies of our cognitive processes and proposed that individuals who do not exhibit a clear preference for either hand are 'mixed-handed.' The research suggests that globally, a significant number of people cannot distinctly identify as either left-hand or right-hand dominant. They may not consistently use one hand for most tasks, nor can they categorize an entire side of their body as dominant or weaker.

Other experts refer to this phenomenon as crossed or mixed laterality, attributing it to a combination of genetic and environmental factors. The fascinating consensus among these experts aligns with a belief I have held for some time: mixed dominance in our body functions is not a disorder. Rather, it represents the diverse ways in which our unique identities manifest. This understanding does not imply that individuals with mixed laterality are exempt from having any disorders, but rather that mixed laterality itself is not inherently a disorder.

Recent studies have in fact shown that children or even adults suffering from development disorders such as attention deficit disorder (ADD) or attention deficit and hyperactivity disorder (ADHD) may be mixed-handed, or they may experience crossed laterality. It could also be that they are just center-brain dominant! It could be that many of the methods being used to reach and teach these individuals are not taking their cross laterality into consideration.

There is no evidence that all persons suffering from ADHD and ADD are mixed or center-brain dominant, neither is every center-brained person also hyperactive or unable to remain focused. Here I am - Exhibit A! Except for that little episode with m-e-n-y, eons ago, that I mentioned before, I was a model student! I now regard that episode as evidence of my center-brained tendency, but I've always been able to stay focused on the task at hand, and to excel academically. I have been described as conscientious, diligent, hardworking by my teachers and supervisors, and sociable, compassionate, a team player, by my peers. Don't get me wrong, I was no pushover. I always was, and still am, very independently minded, but I learned from a very early age that I could disagree with people and still be their friend. So, I certainly was, and still am not someone who was in any way disruptive or discordant.

CHARACTERISTICS OF A CENTER-BRAINED PERSON

It is true that there is, currently, ongoing research into cross laterality, with studies exploring its prevalence, causes and effects on cognition and other functions of the person affected by the condition. But much more needs to be done, especially when we consider how the various manifestations are so person-specific.

Notwithstanding, there are some similarities that can broadly identify persons with center-brained tendencies. Here are some qualities that I have and that I have seen in other individuals whom I find to be center-brained like me:

Balanced Thinking: We are equally skilled in both logical reasoning and creative thinking, as I've mentioned before. We're often able to uncover the logic behind most arguments, even those presented by opponents. We have a natural ability to "fill in the blanks" and "read between the lines" in any situation.

Adaptability: We are able to seamlessly transition between analytical and creative tasks. With the information provided, we can generate well-structured solutions through a combination of innovation and improvisation.

Holistic Problem-Solving: We approach problem solving with both detailed analysis and big-picture thinking. We can simultaneously see both the forest and the trees, allowing us to arrive at one or even multiple solutions, efficiently.

Flexibility: We thrive in both structured settings and in those requiring outside-the-box thinking. While others may be rattled by unforeseen challenges, we remain composed, maintaining focus on the goal—even if it continues to shift.

Effective Communication: We possess solid skills in both verbal and non-verbal communication, excelling particularly in storytelling, which blends logic and creativity. We communicate clearly and effectively, ensuring our message is heard. Many of us are adept at crafting and conveying our own narratives.

If you resonate with even half of these traits, you might just be "center-brained." On an intellectual level, we all have these tendencies to some extent. This may explain why our varying degrees of difficulty at navigating have not been more widely known. Many of us are very skilled at masking or rationalizing our weaknesses.

> *"I always felt something was wrong with my brain...After 50 years of having this and being terrified of driving places (or going to a new building or doctor's appointment, etc.), I found a neighbor that has the same thing and it felt so comforting that I was not the only one! It is a strange thing to have. However, understanding what it is helps in dealing with it."* - Sheila L

While the term "center-brained" is not yet well-known, the idea of a balanced use of both hemispheres of the brain is invaluable. The use of both sides of the brain equally is also referred to as golden brained.

Activities and thinking patterns that integrate both analytical and creative processes can lead to more versatile and adaptive cognitive abilities. It may be that in a center-brained individual, both hemispheres actually cooperate, but it could also mean that many times, they compete. This can lead to a kind of cognitive overload, where the brain is trying to process too much information at once. As a result, the center-brained individual may become more confused than ever, when asked to differentiate left from right or to navigate to a new area. Truth be told, though, we can become confused even while navigating in an area we're supposed to know!

But because we will not be able to readily self-identify as being left-brained or right-brain, we will not appear to naturally adhere to the functions of the right or left hemisphere of the brain, and therefore, are less inclined to exercise one type of thinking over the other. We do have the tendency to be confused by directions that are almost always oriented towards the left-brained, right-hand dominant individual. Being center-brained may also mean that the posterior region of our hippocampus is smaller than that of other individuals. As a consequence, our ability to orient ourselves in space is adversely affected.

If we can verify the foregoing, can we also verify whether the spatial cognition of the center-brained individual can be improved? I definitely believe we can. I also believe our spatial awareness and orientation skills can be enhanced. This is what we will discuss in the next chapter.

10
Sensible coping mechanisms: My perspective

The human brain is a marvel of complexity, capable of process-ing vast amounts of information and performing intricate tasks. However, it is important to recognize that our brains are not identical. While some may excel in certain areas, others may face difficulties with tasks that seem simple, such as distin-guishing left from right or identifying cardinal directions. These challenges do not necessarily signify a cognitive deficiency; rather, they highlight the diverse nature of our neurological makeup. When directional challenges arise, individuals may either independently, or with professional assistance and technological aids, strive to lead normal or near-normal lives. The fact that many more people have not been identified as being directionally challenged demonstrates the fact that some of us whose brains are wired differently, can compensate, and have successfully adopted strategies to enhance their naviga-tional abilities.

Research in this field is still in its early stages, but it is crucial that it be intensified. We need to understand the prevalence of directional disorientation, the various ways it manifests in different individuals, and the coping mechanisms that are currently in use. Additionally, there is a need to raise awareness among those unfamiliar with the condition, and to equip them with the understanding necessary to support affected family members, coworkers, acquaintances, and peers. Enlightenment is required on two fronts: those unaware of spatial or geographic disorientation must learn that it is a genuine condition affecting navigational abilities, while those who are directionally challenged should be informed of the resources and methods available to help them improve their navigational skills.

To each his/her own

What I have learned about myself, and from the numerous directionally challenged individuals with whom I have spoken, is that no two persons are affected in exactly the same way. Therefore:

- It is evident that no single program can universally enhance our ability to distinguish between right and left or improve our navigational skills. Each of us learns and processes information differently, which means a one-size-fits-all approach will be ineffective.
- A significant step towards achieving directional clarity is recognizing that our sense of direction isn't entirely innate. Much of it is acquired through learning, which means that with effort and the right strategies, we have the potential to unlearn our directional inhibitions and improve our spatial awareness and navigational abilities.
- Navigation is a skill that can be honed and improved with practice.

- The key is individualized strategies for each person. I remember that when it was time for me to learn to drive, a group of us – all girls, was being taught by a young man who had a great reputation as a very competent driving instructor. Note that this was in a country, and at a time when almost all vehicles had manual shift gears. But we all did fairly well in guiding the car forward. Two of us – no prizes for guessing who one was – had a tremendous challenge reversing. In fact, that man just gave up on us, saying something like, "Not everyone was born to drive."

As I mentioned previously, it was only when I found myself alone in the car, on an isolated driveway, that I finally began to master the art of reversing. The process was both painstaking and frustrating, but the advantage of solitude was that I had no one to criticize me, except myself. Once I managed to internalize the instructions and could consistently repeat them, after numerous unsuccessful tries, I was finally able to reverse with some degree of confidence. My major challenge was in grasping the concept that when reversing a vehicle, I needed to turn the steering wheel in the opposite direction compared to when driving forward. This realization was crucial for mastering the technique of reversing effectively.

That reminds me of when I was being taught to crochet. I could not hold the needle correctly, and all my effort resulted in a grotesque patchwork of entangled thread. My crochet teacher said I was crocheting left-handed, although I held the needle in my right hand! Only when she gave up, and I sat by myself, read the instructions, and studiously followed them, did I finally learn to crochet. What I did in acquiring both the skills of reversing and crocheting was, I read and understood the instructions, then audibly instructed myself to follow them.

Just as I was able to guide myself into mastering the techniques of reversing and crocheting, I've discovered that engaging in self-dialogue helps me navigate various situations effectively. Whether it's recalling where I parked my car, identifying the correct exit from a building, or determining if I've encountered a particular sign before, this internal conversation often leads me to the right conclusion.

I've realized that I am both an auditory and visual learner. While I rely heavily on visual cues, it's essential for me to hear a verbal explanation that complements the visuals, and this explanation must be coherent and logical.

WHAT I DO

Navigation has certainly come a long way from the days when we relied solely on the sun to orient ourselves during the day, and the stars at night—provided the skies were clear and unobstructed by trees. Today, our smartphones have revolutionized the way we travel, replacing these ancient methods with precise and reliable guidance at our fingertips.

When I say we could have used the sun and the stars, I mean only some of us could, and that would depend on what season it was. I would still have a challenge whether or not it was a cloudless day, because the sun does not exactly rise in the east and set in the west all year round. It's more south-easterly in the winter, and more north-easterly in the summer, in the western hemisphere, that is. Since I don't know where east and west are, a meandering sun will only make navigating more difficult for me.

Before embarking on any journey, I like to familiarize myself with the route well in advance of the actual trip, whether or not I plan to use GPS. Sometimes I do a "dry run" of the route, noting the landmarks, the challenging points - like roundabouts - and most importantly, checking, with the help of the GPS, to see how much time I would need, when the route has far more traffic.

To manage my struggles with navigation and find my way more effectively, I have had to create reliable systems. For instance, when I first moved to Brooklyn, New York, several years ago, I would find myself lost almost every day. My most perplexing ordeal was stepping out of the subway and having absolutely no clue which way to turn to get home. Interestingly, I encountered the same confusion at the start of my journey, but it didn't bother me as much since I wasn't living in Manhattan or Queens. However, not knowing the way home was a different story, and quite unsettling. Despite trying to use signs and landmarks, nothing seemed to help. I continually asked myself, "Was the McDonald's on this side of the street or the other side, when I'm heading home?" The answer depended on which subway exit I emerged from, which, in turn, was influenced by the subway coach I had traveled in.

Over the years, I improved slightly, but it was still a challenge. Eventually, I discovered that by consistently riding in, say, the fifth coach, I could exit the station at the same location each time. As I grew more acquainted with the subway system, I noticed that many others also adhered to this routine. These individuals would prefer to wait for another train rather than compromise on their chosen coach, even at the risk of being late. Insights like these have led me to believe that there are far more people struggling with directional challenges than we realize. At least, those who adopted such routines had crafted a workaround for their navigational difficulties.

In my quest to navigate home after emerging from the subway, I also had to devise a workaround. I began to rely on the buses traveling along the street to guide me. I quickly realized that the destinations displayed on the buses that traveled along my route could serve as a helpful compass. For instance, my journey involved walking along Church Avenue before turning onto the avenue leading to my home. The B35 bus was the only one operating on that section of Church Avenue. Therefore, upon exiting the subway station, I would check the buses traveling on my side of the street. If the bus displayed "McDonald Avenue," I knew I needed to walk in the opposite direction of the bus to reach home. Conversely, if it displayed "Brownsville," I would walk in the same direction as the bus.

Frequently, I would stand at the stop, and await the approaching buses. As they drew near, I carefully read the destination in the front display window. Occasionally, a bus would stop for me, and I would step back apologetically, shaking my head, indicating that I didn't intend to board. I was simply using the bus's route as a navigational tool to determine my path home.

By observing the bus's direction, I could easily deduce my home's location relative to my current position, ensuring I was always on the right track.

Earlier, I shared my method for distinguishing my left hand from my right. For many years, I relied on the image of Teacher Walcott holding a box of chalk in her left hand. This memory served me well whenever I had ample time to think it through, but in more urgent situations, it was less reliable.

Recently, during a conversation with my daughter about our shared difficulties and the strategies we use to overcome them, she introduced me to a much more effective technique for identifying left and right. This method was taught to her by a friend who also struggles with direction. Here it is:

Hold both hands in front of you with your palms facing forward. Notice how the thumb on each hand naturally separates from the other four fingers. This simple positioning will reveal that the thumb and forefinger of your left hand form a properly oriented uppercase 'L.' My daughter shared these instructions over the phone, and with my center- or mixed-brain propensity, I found it very challenging to grasp what she was saying. It took me a long time to understand the clarity of this method. Therefore, I won't try to explain it.

The picture below is worth a thousand words!

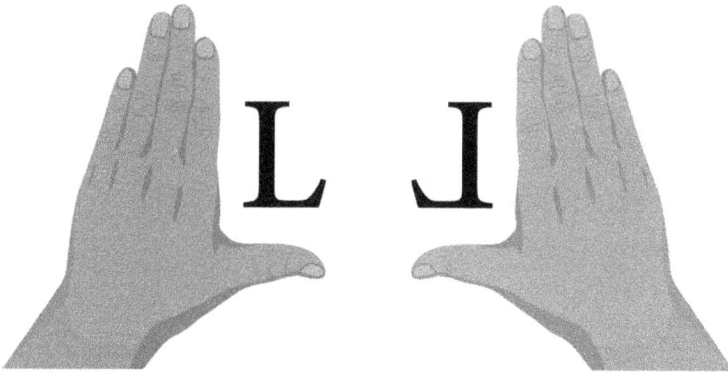

Look at the shape formed by the thumb and forefinger of each hand. The hand that forms a proper upper case "L" is the left hand.

GLOBAL POSITIONING SYSTEM -GPS, YES!

In the days before GPS technology revolutionized navigation, embarking on a journey to an unfamiliar destination in the remote countryside often meant relying on traditional methods of wayfinding. It was not uncommon for me to find myself retracing my steps until I arrived at a location that I recognized.

Once I got back to the familiar, I would recheck the directions, recalibrate my progress, then start again.

This process, though occasionally frustrating, was an integral part of the adventure. If I had the time, I would enjoy the layer of unpredictability and discovery added to each journey.

In addition, without any mechanism to measure the distance I traveled, I was certain that my estimation would be inaccurate. Consequently, I found it incredibly beneficial to encounter markers along expansive country roads. These markers not only indicated when I had reached specific milestones but also divided each mile into eighth segments. This division made it easy to understand that four of these smaller markers equaled half a mile, providing a precise understanding of the distance covered. Even today, when driving along those long back roads, and even with GPS, I have found that using those markers is so much easier than having to glance occasionally at the odometer or the phone, to calculate how far I had progressed.

Let me tell you a fascinating story about a clever little trick I learned before the era of smartphones equipped with GPS applications. A friend of mine once shared a travel tip that was remarkably practical. Before embarking on a journey, she would use MapQuest to generate directions. As she followed these directions, whenever she turned onto a new road, she would reset her car's trip odometer. This allowed her to precisely measure the distance traveled on each segment of her journey. It was an ingenious way to ensure she didn't miss any turns or overshoot the distance she needed to travel, providing peace of mind and accuracy during her trips.

It meant she did not have to do any math! When she demonstrated it to me, it seemed like rocket science!

In today's world, whether you're walking or driving, as long as your phone battery is charged and you have a GPS app installed, finding your way has become remarkably straightforward. The convenience of modern technology means that, with just a functioning device, you can easily navigate your surroundings.

Having access to the internet can significantly enhance your navigation experience, making the process even smoother. It's also worth noting that some GPS applications are designed to function without an internet connection, allowing you to find your way even in remote areas.

I have found that some deep-breathing exercises work wonders for me before I start driving, because when I'm nervous, my breathing tends to become shallow, ergo, less oxygen is taken in; less oxygen goes to my brain, and I'll have a diminished ability to properly make decisions - not a desirable situation while driving. A deliberate effort at being calm will reduce the tendency to be angry either with myself, if I make a mistake, or with others who do crazy things on the road. My calmness will allow me to better cope with traffic jams and other unforeseen hazards, including other drivers.

One thing that I will not do is suddenly swerve from the left to the right in order to make an exit. I try to position myself in or near the exit lanes, at least two miles from my intended exit. If I am unable to make my exit on time, I will calmly pass it, expecting my GPS to reroute me. Doing that is far safer than suddenly cutting across four lanes of traffic.

So, a GPS system can be extremely helpful, but is it the panacea of all directional challenges? Certainly not.

As my husband often remarks, anything crafted by humans is susceptible to mistakes. No frequent GPS user has escaped the occasional bewilderment caused by the perplexing directions offered by our usually reliable digital navigator.

However, overall, this invention has proven to be an invaluable tool, acting as a true lifesaver for many, especially those who struggle with navigation and directional challenges. Its impact on our daily life has been profound. It now offers reassurance and guidance where these were once lacking.

A SOUR NOTE

I would be remiss though, if I did not at least mention one negative effect of GPS use. Christopher Kemp (2020) quotes numerous studies that have found excessive use of GPS to have a deleterious effect on spatial memory.

- Do you recall the groundbreaking study conducted by Dr. McGuire on London taxicab drivers? These drivers, renowned for their exceptional navigational skills, relied solely on their cognitive abilities without the aid of any artificial recording devices. Remarkably, all the intricate data they needed to memorize was stored within their hippocampus. As they mastered the complexities of London's streets, the posterior complex of their hippocampus actually expanded, adapting to accommodate the wealth of additional information.
- Sadly, in a study conducted in 2020 by Louisa Dahmani, a researcher at Harvard College of Medicine, it was found that increased reliance on artificial navigational tools and software significantly diminishes individuals' ability to form mental maps of their surroundings. Despite becoming adept at following a sequence of instructions provided by these technologies, users often miss out on recognizing crucial landmarks, which are essential for developing a comprehensive understanding of their environment (Kemp, 2020).
- Kemp also cited a 2017 study by Hugo Spiers, who used MRI to show the involvement of the hippocampus and

the frontal cortex in navigation, especially when multiple routes were potentially involved. He said brain activity shown on the scanner illustrated the active involvement of the hippocampus, particularly if more than one route was being contemplated, to move from Point A to Point B. However, if GPS is brought into that contingency planning, there is no such brain activity. "When a subject unquestioningly follows a set of given instructions… the hippocampus doesn't perform this act of mental gymnastics. It flat-lines. Silence" (Kemp, 2020, p.176).

Hey! It's important to remember that too much of anything can be detrimental. This is a just gentle reminder to avoid becoming overly dependent on GPS technology. However, there's no doubt about its incredible utility, particularly for those whose hippocampi may have already flat-lined. Use it wisely, and it can be a great ally!

ALTERNATIVE TRANSPORT

If I'm not quite ready to take the wheel for that long road trip, I can still embark on my journey by cab, bus, train, air, or even ferries. These modes of transportation offer valuable opportunities to refine my navigational skills. Mapping my route, observing and comparing landmarks along the way, and jotting down notes provide excellent practice for when I eventually drive myself. Although these alternatives may require more time due to their fixed schedules which are beyond my control, and may necessitate transfers, they can still provide thrilling adventures and important navigational lessons. Disembarking from one unit, and going to find the point of boarding for the next unit can be an entire adventure in and of itself, especially if the incoming unit is behind schedule! With this option, I'll have many opportunities to practice my watch words: Be Calm! Be focused! Be positive!

By using deliberate strategies, we can begin the process towards improving our sense of direction, and thereby, we can change not just our world, but the world at large. If we become more aware, more present, and more connected to the world around us, that, in and of itself, is a form of enlightenment.

The steps I've outlined are vital for individual self-improvement. If those who struggle with directionality unite—embracing our challenges, supporting one another, and collaboratively seeking solutions—our collective potential is boundless.

In the upcoming chapter, let's explore some of the tasks we can undertake together to further this journey.

11
Sensible coping mechanisms: Things we can do together

It's irrefutable that we often find ourselves unable to distinguish our right from our left. Correct? It's also irrefutable that, unlike most other people, we are unable to navigate the world because we struggle to conceptualize our position in relation to others, objects, or locations. So, what steps can we take to address this issue? Unfortunately, many individuals in this situation resign themselves to the belief that they will always struggle with navigation and recognizing directions like left and right. This does not have to be the case. There is encouraging news: the majority of us can develop strategies to mitigate or even overcome these challenges. The fact that this is already happening, is enough evidence that our situation can be improved.

In seeking to identify helpful strategies, it's important to recognize a fundamental truth: the brains of those who are directionally challenged are not naturally wired to easily distinguish between left and right, east and west, or north and south. This is not a flaw but rather a testament to the incredible diversity and adaptability in the composition and function of the human brain. By understanding this fact, we can appreciate the unique ways in which our minds work, and embrace the possibility of developing the strategies we need to navigate the world effectively.

NEURODIVERSITY

Much like the concept of visual reorientation illusion (VRI), the term "neurodiversity" is a relatively new addition to my vocabulary, although I have long championed its principles. Neurodiversity acknowledges the vast array of human cognitive functions and behaviors governed by our brains. It highlights the neurological variations that manifest in human behavior, akin to how ethnicity and gender capture sociological differences in our appearance and actions. This concept spans a range of conditions, not all of which are perceived negatively, and includes individuals who are socially and emotionally well-adjusted as well as those experiencing conditions such as autism, hyperactivity, dyslexia, and geographical disorientation. Moreover, it embraces left-brain dominant, right-brain dominant, and center-brain dominant individuals. From geniuses with exceptionally high IQs to those with cognitive challenges, from overachievers to individuals with developmental delays, from extroverts to those who are socially anxious, and from adventurous nomads capable of traversing great distances to those who feel directionally challenged and hesitant to explore, we are all threads in the intricate tapestry of humanity's neurodiverse landscape.

The term "neurodiversity" emerged in the latter part of the twentieth century, with the intent of ensuring that all individuals in society receive due consideration. Just as advocates for diversity, equity, and inclusion (DEI) assert that all people deserve equal treatment regardless of superficial differences, proponents of neurodiversity argue that every human being occupies a unique position within the expansive realm of typical human behavior. A modicum of recognition has already been given to the fact that some people cannot identify directions and cannot navigate, but the sheer number of individuals who may have no other issue but spatial disorientation, or, who may suffer from other neurological issues, *along with* spatial disorientation, makes it imperative that directional confusion be fully studied. Acknowledging that our navigational abilities can be enhanced is crucial, as this will guide us toward adopting strategies that can facilitate improvement.

SELF-IMPROVEMENT STEPS FOR THE DIRECTIONALLY CHALLENGED

Formal training

At present, there is a noticeable scarcity of training programs specifically designed to enhance spatial orientation skills. However, a few programs do exist that can be quite effective for individuals seeking to improve their navigational abilities. A straightforward internet search using a phrase like "navigation training for the directionally challenged" can yield a variety of potential options. It is evident, nevertheless, that this field is ripe for substantial development and expansion to cater to the growing demand for such training initiatives.

In our pursuit of directional clarity and precision, the starting point of our journey will largely depend on the level of difficulty we face in navigating from Point A to Point B. Whether these points are in separate towns, within a building, or out in the wilderness, each person's approach will be unique. Even when our circumstances appear similar, no two individuals will require the exact same strategies to find their way.

Next, let's challenge our brain.

- Let's try navigating a new route without using a GPS.
- You could also try to go hiking and use a compass to find your way.
- Let others accompany you, and at all times, ensure that your movements and location can be tracked and verified.
- For those who often find themselves on the road, investing in a dedicated GPS navigation device is a wise decision. These devices provide comprehensive navigation features such as lane guidance, real-time traffic updates, and details on nearby points of interest. The most reliable devices operate independently from your car's or smartphone's internet connection, ensuring consistent performance.
- To enhance our navigational skills, let's begin by paying attention to the routes we take in our daily routines. Ask yourself: Which turns lead to my workplace? In which direction is my home from my office? Over time, this practice helps us develop a mental map of our surroundings and create personalized mapping strategies.
- Challenge yourself further by navigating new routes without the aid of a GPS or embark on other hiking adventures using a compass to guide your way. However, it's crucial to have a system in place for monitoring your location and ensuring your safety during these endeavors.
- Eventually, this practice will foster greater confidence in our navigational abilities. From personal experience, I know that if I rely on someone else to drive me around, I am less likely to develop my own driving skills.

Perhaps you have just worked up the courage to learn to drive, or, you want to try again, to obtain your driver's license, after several failed attempts. I have found that getting the vehicle to yourself, in say, an empty parking lot, away from the critical eye of any bystander, including your instructor, and just reading, understanding, and putting into practice, the instructions from the driving manual, can work wonders.

WHERE'S YOUR PHONE?

The phones that we have today can be extremely helpful to the directionally challenged.

Let me say here—and I'm also speaking to myself on this—make a habit of taking your phone with you, whenever you embark on any journey.

- Too many individuals find themselves in tight spots, not just being lost, but being in some sort of danger, and only then do they realize that their phones are in their vehicle or worse, still at home.
- The phones have excellent cameras, to enable us to take pictures of landmarks and other signs, to help us retrace our steps. This is more effective than making mental maps, although, for our own benefit, we really should take mental note of the landmarks. When we retrieve those photographs, there will be no second guessing, which is what we do most of the time.
- If we still have difficulty on our way back, and if we still have phone service, we can send pictures, especially of our current location, to others who can come in search of us, if they are unable to help us navigate over the phone.
- Even after a phone battery has died, or if it's turned off, the phone can still be traced, so make sure that you keep it on your person.

- Landmarks to photograph while we're on a trip in the countryside include outstanding structures such as rivers, creeks, lakes, strange trees, monuments, unique buildings, bridges, etc. These pictures will be invaluable for later reference.

The foregoing facts significantly enhance the likelihood for those of us who are directionally challenged to either successfully navigate our way or be located before any potential disaster occurs.

Given our tendency to become lost and disoriented, it is truly fortunate that our smartphones possess the capability to share our location. While this feature might be seen as a nuisance by those who are adept navigators and wish to maintain their privacy, it serves as a crucial tool for individuals who struggle with finding their way. Therefore, in addition to verbally informing at least one other person of our intended destination, it is prudent to establish a mutual agreement for some degree of location sharing. This not only ensures our safety but also provides peace of mind for both ourselves and those who care about us.

USING AUGMENTED REALITY (AR) TO NAVIGATE

Many automotive companies and various businesses are now embracing the cutting-edge technology of augmented reality (AR) to enhance their vehicles and devices, and to elevate their sales promotions. This innovative approach is revolutionizing the industries by offering customers a more immersive and interactive experience. AR is technology that connects the physical world with an entirely digital or virtual environment.

For those who struggle with directions, this advancement is particularly transformative. Imagine having a 3-Dimensional view of a product you intend to buy, seamlessly integrated into your actual physical environment, allowing you to visualize its application before making a purchase. AR in navigation offers a similar groundbreaking benefit, providing users with a more intuitive and engaging way to get from point A to point B.

- It will also be able to give you a 3-D look at your route and your destination.
- It can allow the directionally challenged to overlay specific objects such as pictures over real-life objects. In a big building, or shopping mall, or city, for example, you would be able to use AR to help you navigate from one place to the next.

This technology helps with visual orientation—something we all lack—and allows us to use our cameras and added instruction to navigate. The AR technology is still being worked on, but it will present endless possibilities to those who frequently get lost, even in familiar surroundings.

THINGS WE MUST DO

At least try

It is too easy for the directionally challenged to decide beforehand, that we will not be able to competently complete a journey, that somewhere along the way, we will get lost, or encounter some insurmountable difficulty.

- We may even decide, beforehand, to not embark on the journey. However, what the study of the London Taxi drivers has taught me is that with practice, our navigational skill will improve.
- What I also know is that far more people than will self-identify, have directional challenges. The reason we don't realize that many of the people we know are also directionally challenged is, they have honed skills that allow them to mitigate the effect of their challenges, with varying degrees of success.
- We all can do that.

Keep in mind that we are likely to lose our way at least once or twice. However, each moment of disorientation will not only sharpen our navigational skills but also allow us to discover a multitude of new places that we would ordinarily overlook. Whenever I find myself lost and need to navigate back, I make a point to take note of all the unfamiliar locations I encounter along the way—places I would never have seen had I not strayed from my intended path.

Plan ahead

One of the major things we need to do is to plan ahead for any trip.

- Also, create a detailed itinerary of your trip. Make it manageable. It's better to over-perform than to fall short of your goals.
- Long gone are the days when we only had paper maps. Gone are the days when we would MapQuest our trip on the computer, but we still had to bring along the printed

instructions - which were admittedly, far superior to the paper maps we used to buy at gas stations.

- The GPS app on our phone today can map out our trip before we leave our driveway, and there are so many types of apps for navigation now available. My preference is for Waze, which gives, along with the standard directions, current information from other road users. But there are other great ones too. By typing in our destination and clicking "Let's Go!" or "Go Now!" then tracing the journey with our fingers, we can note every twist and turn; every landmark and road sign, before we start driving.
- Make a note of these landmarks, and look out for them as you actually travel. This will assure you that you're on the right track.
- Once you have traced all the way to your destination, reset the GPS for "Home" - your address.
- For the return leg, make a note of the landmarks, as they may be different, but whether or not they are, they can appear different to folks like us.
- A very useful feature of the modern GPS is that we can download the map that we'll need and have it accessible at all times, even if we're in an area where internet service is intermittent.
- Google Maps also offers step by step directions and even timely traffic updates.
- The onX Backcountry and Offroad systems as well as others like them can be great for areas where there is no internet service.

Note your turns

Traveling on long, relatively lonely country roads is comparatively easy. We just have to note our exits.

- It is absolutely crucial to avoid making a wrong turn on these remote roads, where petrol stations are scarce and widely dispersed. Running out of fuel in an unfamiliar area is a situation best avoided, as it can lead to significant inconvenience and potential danger.
- In a big city, one of the factors to especially observe is which roads will suddenly turn into one-way traffic lanes, or roads that will temporarily be blocked.
- More importantly, just to be on the safe side, trace one or two alternative routes, so that you will not be totally flustered if you have to detour.
- Of course, the golden rule for the directionally challenged is, we must never go anywhere alone, if we can get someone to go with us. Having a traveling companion, someone who is empathetic, pays rich dividends. Having someone to converse with can allow us to not obsess so much about our driving. We can ask our passenger to look out for signs for us, and if we take a wrong turn, or something else goes wrong, both driver and passenger/navigator can brainstorm solutions.

Now, the foregoing advice pertains only to a road trip. When planning an adventurous journey into the outback, remote bushlands, or along a rugged mountain trail, it is crucial to undertake such an expedition with a substantial group.

- If someone in the group has any kind of mishap and has to return, it is certainly advisable that everybody returns. It is strongly recommended that the whole team returns, the injured party recuperates and the team makes the trip at another time. This approach is significantly safer than having a few individuals, or even just one person, choose to continue or head back alone, potentially leading to a separation from the group and the risk of them becoming lost or isolated indefinitely.
- Always keep in mind what you're currently doing. For example, you're going towards Exit 102, Brown's Creek Road N, or Exit 103, Brown's Creek Road S. The exit is half a mile away. That is what you should be thinking of - not what you'll be doing in an hour. And keep telling yourself that it will all be fine; even if you're currently off course.
- Panicking and giving up will get us nowhere, and may cause us to be involved in an accident.

Quick tips

- Stay attentive while driving, maintaining focus on the traffic and road conditions around you. This vigilance is crucial for ensuring a safe journey.
- Avoid succumbing to the temptation of speeding, but also ensure you do not become a hazard by driving excessively slowly. Strive for a balanced speed that aligns with the flow of traffic.
- If you're uncertain about optimal driving techniques, consider enrolling in a defensive driving course. This education will equip you with the skills to anticipate and respond to various road scenarios, enhancing both your safety and confidence.

- Always verify the GPS instructions with your own observations and pre-planned routes. GPS systems can often alter paths due to real-time traffic updates or accidents, so being aware of these changes is essential.
- Don't be alarmed if your GPS recalculates a new route. It might be doing so to help you avoid traffic delays or other road issues. Preparing at least one alternative route beforehand is a wise strategy.
- If you struggle with navigation, refrain from using your phone for calls or texts while driving. Only use it for receiving driving instructions. If an urgent need to communicate arises, safely pull over to a secure location to make calls or send texts before rejoining the flow of traffic.

Review, review, review!

As we go about planning our trip, we must make certain to plan for time to review:

- when we can stop and assess the ground we've covered
- what we'll see
- how well we're progressing, and
- how much further we have to go.

It's much better to give yourself more time than you need, to cover the distance, then to force yourself to cover a longer distance when you're tired. If it is at all practicable - the destination is not too far - doing a trial run would be an excellent idea. I remember the many times I needed to be at a new location early on a Monday morning, for example, and I would make the journey Sunday evening. I only needed to make allowance for extra traffic when I made the trip again the following morning.

- Also, if you're like me you will want to check the weather forecast, just so that you will not be driving in a heavy downpour.
- It's never wise to start your mission to navigational acuity by making a long journey. Let your prowess and confidence levels rise each time, by first making small trips, then assessing your progress, and venturing further and further, from the familiar.

If the journey is going to take several days, plan to drive during the day, and rest at nights. Check into a small hotel along the way and completely relax. Night driving presents additional challenges that we might want to eliminate at the beginning of our journey to navigational prowess.

JUST DO IT!

When doing the actual trip, it goes without saying that the vehicle must be in tip top shape with our gas tank full; and we should follow the instructions from our GPS.

- Begin your journey promptly, or even ahead of schedule if possible. Doing so will help alleviate the anxiety that naturally builds up during travel.
- Keep an eye out for and take note of previously identified landmarks. These familiar markers can serve as reassuring guides along your route.
- If you find yourself uncertain about directions, don't hesitate to pause and inquire for help. Ensure you

stop at safe, reputable locations and seek advice from individuals who are likely knowledgeable about the area. Delivery drivers from companies like UPS and FedEx, as well as mail carriers, are often reliable sources of information. If they are unfamiliar with the location you're asking about, they are typically honest about it and can direct you to someone who can assist. Be cautious when asking locals who may travel the route frequently but have never consciously thought about the directions, as they might inadvertently mislead you.

- As you travel, use your GPS and ask for directions, make a conscious effort to memorize as much of the route as possible. Cross-check these mental notes with the directions you receive to ensure accuracy.
- The ultimate goal throughout your journey is to enhance your ability to create and retain mental maps, thus improving your navigational skills.

With each successful trip, try to rely, even ever so slightly, less on the GPS and more on your memory. Remember the capacity of the posterior hippocampus can be increased.

The bottom line on any trip is to stay calm, stay focused, and stay positive. These states of mind will be fully mastered only after consistent practice, but we should all be aiming for them, at all times.

Finally, embrace the power of mindfulness.

- Be present in the moment and fully engage with your surroundings.
- Notice the position of the sun, the direction of the wind, the layout of the streets; the colors and sizes of the

buildings, the shapes and height of the trees and other natural structures.

- At first, if you know you will not remember, keep a journal; one that chronicles the steps you take on any journey - short or long; in a vehicle or on foot. And always remember to outline the return leg of the journey as well. When I moved from Brooklyn, New York, to Palm Bay, Florida, I left a situation in which trains, buses, taxis - official and unofficial - were within easy reach, to a situation where I had to drive. I wrote down all the routes I used and that really helped.

Eventually, you will be able to rely mostly on yourself. That is the goal. The more we try to navigate on our own, the better we'll become at doing it.

Moreover, engaging in cognitive exercises can significantly enhance the brain's ability to comprehend and follow directions. These exercises might include solving puzzles, playing video games, and participating in certain physical activities that demand spatial awareness. It's important to emphasize that this isn't about 'fixing' something that's 'broken' or 'defective'. Instead, it's about understanding the unique ways our brains function and discovering methods to expand our ability to navigate the world more effectively.

If you were wondering, "Is there any help for me?" you should know the answer by now. It's a resounding Yes! As we've explored, there are numerous resources, strategies, and technologies designed to address and improve our directional challenges. It's crucial to increase awareness of these challenges and put forth a concerted effort to acknowledge and mitigate them.

The foregoing factors give the directionally challenged a better chance of either finding the way, or being found, before a disaster happens. Our final chapter will delve into how the world can assist us in overcoming the obstacles we face.

12
Achieving directional enlightenment: Let's change the world!

Do you now agree that experiencing directional confusion is not necessarily a reflection of one's intelligence or level of education? If this resonates with you, it's likely you also have some insight into the potential causes. Regardless of why you, I, or anyone else might struggle to navigate from one location to another, it is important to recognize that we are not destined to lose our way every time we set out on a journey. Many techniques are available that can significantly enhance our navigational abilities, allowing us to lead lives that are nearly indistinguishable from the lives of those who naturally find their way with ease. However, our personal efforts alone might not suffice. Society can also play a role by adopting strategies that help accommodate the unique issues faced by those who are directionally challenged. By doing so, we can foster a more understanding and tolerant environment for everyone. These strategies should be implemented by:

- the people with whom we often interact
- businesses and commercial services providers

- health care providers
- social services providers
- educators
- the scientific community and
- government agencies,

to first of all, recognize that a large swathe of the human population can be categorized as directionally challenged - or whatever label is finally decided on; and we require

- acknowledgement - self-identification
- recognition
- acceptance
- more study
- more accommodation,
- new attitudes
- new devices
- new policies
- even new legislation.

When I embarked on this journey of self-exploration and discovery, I believed I was just an ordinary person with an extraordinary brain that functions differently. Through my research into the phenomenon of being directionally challenged, I have uncovered and shared numerous insights with you. My findings have not only broadened my under-standing but have also reinforced my belief in the normality of our condition. It's evident that those who are just discovering the world of the directionally challenged will need to adjust to this "new normal." Despite this, I am optimistic and assured that society can and will accommodate this change.

WHAT CAN WE DO?

Reflecting on past regulations that have been implemented to support individuals requiring special considerations offers valuable insights. Consider the scenario of a typical woman employed outside her home who discovers she is expecting a child. Less than a century ago in the United States, such a woman could potentially have faced job loss upon revealing her pregnancy. If fortunate enough to retain her position until childbirth, she would often be compelled to resume work almost immediately, as the absence of paid maternity leave necessitated a quick return. We've come a long way on this issue, and thankfully, significant progress has been made, to be more responsive to the needs of this particular cohort of the population that needed due consideration.

The concept of paid maternity leave gained global acceptance in the 20th century, even though the U.S. was notably among the last group of developed nations to adopt such policies. The Family and Medical Leave Act (FMLA) of 1993 marked a milestone by offering eligible employees 12 weeks of *unpaid* leave. Typically, pregnant women must determine the extent of unpaid leave they can afford unless their employer provides paid leave. Recent developments have also recognized the importance of paternity leave, acknowledging the advantages of both parents being available to support the newborn's optimal development.

Obviously, pregnancy is not a permanent condition. Being directionally challenged doesn't need to be a permanent label either. Through extensive observation and research, compelling evidence suggests that directional confusion can be alleviated, if not entirely resolved, provided that all parties involved are committed to making the necessary effort.

I concede that if the directional confusion is caused by serious physiological deficiencies, then a complete reversal may not be possible, but much can be done for individuals who can be retrained to regard their spatial orientation from different perspectives.

So, what exactly is needed?

- The first step is for those adults who know that they are directionally confused to stop being ashamed; to own their condition, and find ways to overcome their challenges.
- Parents, guardians and custodians of directionally challenged children should identify the characteristic in their children and seek to access facilities and professionals who understand the condition and are prepared to work with the directionally challenged.

SOCIAL SERVICES PROVIDERS

Here are some of the ways in which the providers of social services can assist the directionally challenged:

Public Awareness - They must understand that there is an urgent need to raise public awareness about the directional and navigational difficulties that a substantial segment of the population experiences. An educational campaign must be designed to empower individuals who face these challenges, to motivate them to seek appropriate interventions and accommodations. This campaign should seek to enlighten the broader community about the hurdles their peers encounter, thereby cultivating a more understanding and supportive environment. By enhancing awareness and fostering empathy, we can work towards a society that acknowledges and addresses these challenges more effectively.

Policy and Advocacy – Social services providers must make every effort to advocate for the directionally challenged, to promote their optimal involvement in the day-to-day activities of society, such as education, employment, transportation and the use of public spaces.

Accessibility Assessments - Social services providers need to:

- Educate themselves about this condition
- Seek to sensitize the society to what is occurring, and what needs to be done
- Carry out assessments of the different environments of the directionally challenged - the home, school, workplace, public places, transportation options, etc., to identify the factors that foster directional and navigational confusion
- Make recommendations that can inform other members of the society.

Training, Education, Counseling - Social services providers can:

- Provide programs aimed at enhancing spatial and navigational skills, especially for adults. These programs should incorporate firsthand experience of those who have successfully dealt with their directional challenges
- Provide counseling services and support groups to teach coping skills
- Provide access to assistive technology-based navigational aids
- Identify specialized services for further assessment and targeted interventions.

EDUCATORS

Professional Development - In order to properly cater to this newly recognized group, educators must seek to further develop and widen their own teaching skills, to allow them to better assist the directionally challenged students. They must collaborate with the scientific community to help develop the requisite knowledge and skills base they will need.

Here are some of the ways educators can play a crucial role in fostering greater navigational skills (left vs right, north, south, east and west) in students:

Awareness and Understanding - Educators should:

- Display a greater sensitivity to the challenges faced by children with directional confusion
- Understand that students with directional confusion are not stupid or lazy. They genuinely have a problem identifying their right and their left, and the cardinal points
- Create teaching and support strategies to more effectively deal with their directionally challenged students.

Visual Aids and Mapping - It is much easier nowadays, than it was in the past, to access visual and other aids for use with students who are directionally challenged. Their use of clear, level-specific and appealing visual aids, enhanced by modern technology, can assist in making spatial relationships more realistic.

Explicit Instructions with Verbal Cues - In teaching-learning situations, teachers need to:

- Provide clear and explicit verbal and other type of instructions to assist students in understanding what they need to do, where they need to go, and how to get there

- Help the students who cannot identify left and right, by providing strategies such as the left-hand clue mentioned in Chapter 10
- Start reorientation strategies for the young directionally challenged child, as early as possible
- Make available conspicuously placed copies of site maps, with clear directions, including arrows and prominent landmarks on the school campus, especially in each classroom, to help reinforce navigational skills.

Catering to Different Learning Styles - Educators can introduce alternative navigation instructions that cater to different learning styles and abilities. The strategies to be introduced may include auditory cues, tactile markers, or technology-based devices such as global positioning systems - GPS, and smartphone apps.

Structured Learning Environments
- The establishment of structured routines and classroom layouts can help directionally challenged students to feel more comfortable and confident in their learning environment.
- There should be every effort to minimize changes in the physical layout of the classrooms, to reduce confusion in the students.
- To begin, dedicated classrooms for directionally challenged students, to which teachers will go, instead of having the students move from classroom to classroom will reduce their anxiety. Students should then be taught to gradually use the navigational skills they are learning to go to other areas of the school campus.

Peer Support and Collaboration - Educators should Encourage optimal peer support and collaboration, to assist students with directional challenges. These students can be paired with students who are adept at finding their way around, for their mutual benefit, especially so that the students who are not directionally challenged may gain an understanding of what the directionally challenged experience.

Individualized Instruction - Every effort should be made to provide individualized learning programs that specifically address the needs of students with directional challenges. These programs may include particular strategies, accommodations and goals related to spatial and navigation skills.

THE SCIENTIFIC AND HEALTH CARE COMMUNITY

Ways in which the scientific community can help the directionally challenged include:

Research and Understanding - Scientists must conduct greater research to better appreciate the difficulties we experience, and the neurological and cognitive mechanisms underlying our spatial orientation. A proper understanding of causes, variations in effects and also effective interventions will greatly help each cohort to learn about this condition and how to deal with it.

Diagnostic Tools and Assessment - Their research must determine new and improved diagnostic tools as well as assessment methodologies to facilitate early diagnosis of spatial and navigational challenges, leading to timely interventions and strategies geared at dealing with the needs of the directionally challenged.

Technological Innovations - The participation of the scientific community is vital in the development of assistive technologies and tools such as the GPS mentioned before, virtual reality (VR) training programs or smartphone apps, to help the directionally challenged.

Intervention Strategies - Ongoing studies are necessary, to evaluate the effectiveness of the interventions being used. These interventions will include cognitive training programs, behavioral therapies, even the strategies employed by educators, all in an effort to fine-tune evidence-based practices for supporting individuals who experience spatial and navigational challenges.

Collaboration with Other Disciplines - The scientific community encompasses experts from fields such as psychology, neuroscience, education and engineering. These disciplines must all work together to devise holistic and integrated solutions to the problems faced by the directionally challenged.

Training for Health and Other Professionals - Enhanced training is needed for healthcare professionals, educators, commercial and social services providers to enable them to better support individuals with directional challenges, by providing effective care and accommodations.

GOVERNMENT

Government agencies must:

- Take a leading role in fostering a better living, learning and working environment for the directionally challenged, in engendering changes in attitudes, practices and products, through legislation, policies, initiatives and support programs

- Encourage public and private agencies to devise programs and strategies, to help the directionally challenged better navigate within their environment.

Legislation and Policy Development - Governments will be well advised to initiate feasibility studies into the passage of legislation dealing with the categorization of the directionally challenged, and the rights and amenities that should lawfully be theirs, in all aspects of their lives.

Although I am of the firm opinion that the directionally challenged individual is not a disabled person, I believe that we can be rendered powerless by directions that are not clear to us, and by the attitudes of persons with whom we have to interact, who do not understand our situation. Therefore, one body of legislation from which tenets of laws favoring the directionally challenged could be garnered is the Americans with Disabilities Act (ADA) of 1990, as well as some of its precursors - the Individuals with Disabilities Education Act (IDEA) of 1975 and the Air Carrier Access Act (ACAA) of 1986, plus, some later legislations such as the 21st Century Communications and Video Accessibility Act (CVAA) of 2010, and the Workforce Innovation and Opportunity Act (WIOA) of 2014.

The laws favoring the directionally challenged will aim to provide greater accommodation and inclusion for us, as well as to allow us the freedom to be ourselves, without the threat of condemnation, termination or ostracization.

Accessibility Regulations - Governments can enact and enforce rules and regulations that mandate greater and more explicit site maps in public places, on public transportation, bus stops and depots, and at subway stations, to facilitate the directionally challenged. The floors, walls, or ceilings of subway stations, for example, could be painted with arrows leading to the various trains and exits, as well as the names of streets that are easily accessible from each exit.

- They could require large plazas and stores to install additional site maps to assist visitors in navigating their premises more easily. These entities could be encouraged to develop user-friendly mobile applications, accessible by scanning a QR code, to offer personalized guidance and enhance the overall experience for those who find directional navigation challenging when visiting their locations. They might even be encouraged to employ wardens to direct motorized and foot traffic on their premises.
- Some effort would also have to be made to make road, especially highway signs more centrally placed, to make them more visually accessible to the directionally challenged.

Education and Awareness Campaigns - Government is also expected to spearhead public awareness campaigns about the difficulties experienced by the directionally challenged; to initiate their own campaigns, as well as to encourage and help sponsor similar campaigns within the private sector.

Funding for Research and Development - Again, Governments would be expected to provide a major portion of the incentives for scientific research, for technological development and for training of personnel, to improve available navigational aids and to invent news ones, as well as assistive technologies and intervention strategies for individuals with directional challenges.

Public Health Support - Governments must lead the way in facilitating the diagnosis, treatment and follow-up support of the directionally challenged. They must recognize and allow health insurance coverage for the requisite assessments, therapies and assistive devices that will be required to assist the directionally challenged.

Employment and Other Programs - The ultimate aim is for the directionally challenged to live as near-normal lives as possible. However, for some, and for others - at least at the beginning - the government could implement programs that promote training and job opportunities that do not require a great deal of navigation and spatial acuity.

Collaboration with All Stakeholders - While it is in the best interest of all other stakeholders to work collaboratively to alleviate the problems of the directionally challenged, government agencies will be especially charged with:

- Facilitating the interactions between all the groups tasked with improving the lot of the directionally challenged
- Co-opting the assistance of disability advocacy groups and optimizing the input of groups such as healthcare professionals, nursing and medical schools, educators and teacher training institutions, researchers, manufacturers, technology developers, captains of industry, business operators
- Making every effort to facilitate the provision of the requisite resources - manpower and financial, that they are best suited to provide.

The problems faced by those who are directionally challenged may not seem significant to others, but for those affected, we face a daily struggle filled with trauma, shame, and fear. Every day demands the daunting task of explaining why simple, routine activities that others take for granted are either impossible for us or require an inordinate amount of time. Most of us are generally competent drivers, yet our anxiety and difficulty with navigation can pose risks not only to ourselves but also to other road users.

Gaining a deeper understanding of our situation and being informed about its implications are crucial to the creation of effective solutions to our dilemma. As the adages wisely remind us: *A problem shared is a problem halved* and *The first step towards solving a problem is a proper understanding of it*. I hope that through this effort, I have successfully highlighted the issues that are peculiar to us, and illuminated the nature and extent of these issues. Hopefully, you've identified your role in the tasks that all must undertake, and you are eager to help accomplish them. Now, let's go change the world!

Afterword

Everyone must, after reading this book, be alerted to the urgent need for mobilized action against a situation that has disadvantaged a wide cross-section of the world's population. The inability of millions of people to competently navigate spatially has caused them to be mischaracterized and deprived of many social interactions because of their reticence to engage in activities that involve navigating from one point to another.

The time has come for every society to acknowledge and address the unique needs of citizens who experience directional challenges. It is crucial for individuals who identify as directionally challenged to acknowledge their condition, and for all stakeholders to come together to form a coalition committed to transformative change. This coalition should spearhead efforts to dismantle the unwarranted stigma associated with being directionally challenged and advocate for the creation of a more inclusive society. This will entail designing tools, devices, and everyday objects that cater to a diverse range of users, rather than predominantly favoring right-handed individuals.

This is a clarion call to action for everyone to get involved. If you identify as directionally challenged, seize this moment to become an active participant in the movement. If you are directionally proficient, reflect on the significant impact you can make by supporting this cause. Let us work together to ensure that future generations will be thankful for our dedication to creating a world that is more navigable and accommodating for all citizens!

Sign up for updates on the movement! We'll find each other no matter where we end up . . .

https://www.epatsygreenland.com/

Glossary

A

Absent-minded professor – Someone who is highly intellectual; can contemplate complex ideas, but is unable to carry out simple functions, like wearing matching socks, or navigating from Point A to Point B. See https://www.phrases.org.uk/meanings/absent-minded-professor.html#google_vignette. Page 24

Agenesis of the corpus callosum (ACC) – A birth defect in the brain. The corpus callosum, a bundle of nerves connecting the left and right hemispheres of the brain, is either totally or partially missing. Symptoms of ACC include minor intelligence issues and developmental delays, as well as seizures. ACC is usually diagnosed in the first two years of life. https://my.clevelandclinic.org/health/diseases/6029-agenesis-of-the-corpus-callosum-acc. Page 39

Anathema – Something that is intensely disliked, loathed or cursed. https://www.merriam-webster.com/dictionary/anathema. Page 15

Attention deficit disorder (ADD) – An inability of the brain to develop optimally. It is manifested in inattentiveness and impulsiveness. Since 1994, US doctors decreed that this term would no longer be used. Page 95

Attention deficit and hyperactivity disorder (ADHD) – An inability of the brain to develop optimally. It is manifested in inattentiveness, impulsiveness and hyperactivity. Since 1994, US doctors decreed that this term would be used to describe all attention-deficit issues, even if the person was not hyperactive. Affected persons are now described as having ADHD – Inattentive type, ADHD – Hyperactive/Impulsive type, or ADHD – Combined type. https://www.webmd.com/add-adhd/childhood-adhd/add-vs-adhd. Page 95

Augmented Reality (AR) - The integration of digital information with the user's environment in real time. Unlike virtual reality (VR), which creates a totally artificial environment, AR users experience a real-world environment with generated perceptual information overlaid on top of it. https://www.techtarget.com/whatis/definition/augmented-reality-AR. Page 116

Axon – A usually long and single nerve-cell process that usually conducts impulses away from the cell body. https://www.merriam-webster.com/dictionary/axon. Page 38

B

Baff-handed - Appearing to be extremely awkward in accomplishing hand tasks. Usually a description of left-handed persons, when seen from the perspective of a right-handed person. South-paw. #Jamaica https://t.co/EdflLRrPUQ. twitter.com/wiwords/status/876622341685616640?lang=en. Page 35

Brain hemispheres – The human brain is divided into symmetrical left and right sides or hemispheres. Each hemisphere is in charge of the opposite side of the body, so your right brain hemisphere controls your left side. The left brain hemisphere also takes in sensory input from your right side and vice versa. https://www.webmd.com/brain/the-difference-between-the-left-and-right-brain.

(ii) The parts of the brain that control muscle functions, also control speech, thought, emotions, reading, writing, and, learning. The right hemisphere controls the muscles on the left side of the body, and the left hemisphere controls the muscles on the right side of the body. https://www.cancer.gov/publications/dictionaries/cancer-terms/def/cerebral-hemisphere. Page 32

Body-specific hypothesis – The theory that people with different kinds of bodies think differently, in particular, that left-handers and right-handers use different parts of their brains to perceive and conceptualize. https://psycnet.apa.org/record/2011-28626-007. Page 33

C

Cardinal points – The four main directions on a compass – north, south, east, and west, commonly denoted by their initial letters – N, S, E, W. https://www.merriam-webster.com/dictionary/cardinal%20point. Page 17

Center-brained – The notion that instead of having one or the other hemisphere of the brain as dominant, an individual can be governed only by the center of the brain – where the coordination takes place anyway, or by the integrative action of the left, center, and right regions of the brain. Page 2

Cochlea - A spiral liquid-filled tube, approximately 30 mm in length, located in the inner ear. It is vital to the sense of hearing. https://www.verywellhealth.com/cochlea-anatomy-5069393. Page 72

Cognitive functions – Mental processes facilitating the accomplishment of activities we carry out. They include attention, orientation, memory, language, and visual and spatial skills. https://neuronup.us/areas-of-intervention/cognitive-functions/. Page 32

Corpus Callosum – Approximately 200 million heavily sheathed nerve fibers that connect the left and right hemispheres. It integrates and transfers information from one hemisphere to the other, allowing them to process sensory, motor and cognitive signals. https://www.ncbi.nlm.nih.gov/books/NBK448209/. Page 38

Crossed or mixed laterality – A state of not having a dominant hand, foot, eye or ear. It is manifested in the dominance being shared on either side. Studies suggest that mixed laterality does not affect and is not affected by intelligence or academic performance. https://www.ncbi.nlm.nih.gov/pmc/articles/PMC5573212/. Page 95

D

Developmental delays – A series of conditions denoting an impairment in the ability of a child to manifest timely, or any advancement in physical, learning, language and behavioral growth. https://www.cdc.gov/child-development/about/developmental-disability-basics.html. Page 112

Developmental Topographical Disorientation (DTD) – The inability of a person to build up a memory bank of images pertaining to his or her environment and experiences, and therefore the inability to navigate using external cues. DTD is not caused by congenital or imposed brain injury. https://www.ncbi.nlm.nih.gov/pmc/articles/PMC8267524/. Page 64

Directional dyslexia –Since dyslexia is concerned with the inability to decipher and distinguish letters and words, and to follow left to right progression, directional dyslexia could broadly be seen as the inability to decipher, distinguish, and follow a sequence of directions. https://www.dyslexia-reading-well.com/directional-dyslexia.html. Page 56

Directionally challenged – Being unable to differentiate left from right and to identify the cardinal or other points on a compass. https://www.reddit.com/r/AskReddit/comments/iwgmm/what_does_it_really_mean_to_be_directional-ly/?rdt=47142. Page 1

Directional confusion – Same as being directionally challenged. Page 3

Directional disorientation – Same as being directionally challenged and directionally confused. Page 2

Dyslexia – "Dyslexia is a specific learning disability that is neuro-biological in origin. It is characterized by difficulties with accurate and/or fluent word recognition and by poor spelling and decoding abilities. These difficulties typically result from a deficit in the phonological component of language that is often unexpected in relation to other cognitive abilities and the provision of effective classroom instruction. Secondary consequences may include problems in reading compre-hension and reduced reading experience that can impede growth of vocabulary and background knowledge." https://dyslexiaida.org/definition-of-dyslexia/. Page 52

Dysorientia – Inability to use internal mental maps and external visual clues to determine where one has been, where one currently is located, and the next step to take, in order to arrive at a particular destination. Page 77

F

Factory reset – Usually used with electronic devices. Having all memory erased so that the device is as it was when it was just manufactured. Individual suffering from developmental topographical disorientation (DTD) feel like their memory is often erased, since there is no memory of where they been; they cannot identify where they currently are; and they don't know where to go next. Page 16

Flat-line – To die. Refers to the image created by an electrocar-diogram to show heart activity. When the line goes flat the patient is heart-dead –one of the ways used by medical science to determine death. Page 109

G

Geographic dyslexia – Same as directional dyslexia. Page 64

Golden brained – Term used to describe the use of both sides of the brain equally. Similar to being center-brained. A holistic, integrative approach to the functioning of the hemispheres of the brain. https://scc.sa.utoronto.ca/content/the-science-behind-the-left-and-right-brain/. Page 97

H

Handedness – The propensity to use one hand to carry out the most important functions. https://www.merriam-webster.com/dictionary/handedness. Page 29

Hemisphere – Half of a space or area. The prefix "hemi" means half. Sphere usually refers to a roundish form, such as the brain. https://www.merriam-webster.com/dictionary/hemisphere. Page 32

Hemispherectomy – Surgical removal of one side of the brain, or surgical incision that partially or totally removes the corpus callosum, thereby disconnecting the right from the left hemisphere. https://my.clevelandclinic.org/health/procedures/17092-hemispherectomy. Page 75

Hippocampus – A small, seahorse-shaped brain structure, is fundamentally involved in learning, memory formation and spatial navigation. https://www.ncbi.nlm.nih.gov/pmc/articles/PMC3548359/. Page 73

I

Inner Ear – Located in the innermost section of the ear, comprised on two main parts – the cochlea and the semicircular canals, the inner ear is mostly involved the essence of hearing, and, with balance. It works with the brain, and the motor system to help with positioning of the head in movement. https://med.uth.edu/orl/online-ear-disease-photo-book/chapter-3-ear-anatomy/ear-anatomy-inner-ear/. Page 72

K

Kinesthesia – The sense of orientation of the neighboring parts of the body. It allows you to walk without consciously thinking about where to place your foot next. It lets you touch your elbow with your eyes closed. It's present in every muscle you have. Also known as proprioception. Page 74

L

Left-brain-dominant – The notion – not very established – that the left side of the brain is dominant. The dominance of the left hemisphere is allied with the dominance use of the right side and the right hand, etc. https://healthnile.com/quiz/left-brain-right-brain-test/?utm_source=google&utm_medium. Page 68

Left-hand-dominant - Being able to do most activities, most notably, writing, with the left hand. https://www.webmd.com/brain/ss/slideshow-left-handed-vs-right. Page 89

Left hemisphere (of the Brain) – The left side of the brain. Page 32

Left-side-dominant – Using the organs on the left side to carry out the most important functions. For example, using the left hand to write, the left leg to kick, the left ear to hear better, the left eye to see better. Left side dominance is allied to right brain dominace.

M

Mental mapping – Being able to internally produce, store and recall images of the environment in which we exist and move, to enable us to remember where we were, move from where we are, to where we want to go. https://mentalmap.org/mi-a-mentalis-terkepezes/ Page 69

Mixed brained – Evidence that an individual does not receive definite instructions from the brain about which side or hand to use for most functions. https://www.brainbalancecenters.com/blog/mixed-dominance-and-developmental-delay

Mixed-handed – Using either hand to do a major activity. For example, a mixed handed person could use the right hand to write; and toss a ball with the left hand. https://www.brainbalancecenters.com/blog/mixed-dominance-and-developmental-delay. Page 94

Motor system – Comprised of the brain, the spinal column, and the neurons that connect these structures to the muscular skeletal system, this is the section of the neurological system that controls voluntary movement. https://www.getbodysmart.com/motor-system/. Page 72

N

Navigation – The method of being able to determine current location, to be able to identify locations already passed, and to chart a course for where to go next. https://www.merriam-webster.com/dictionary/navigation. Page 3

Nerd – A younger version of the absent-minded professor. Someone, usually young, who is obsessed with whatever may be the interest, to the exclusion of other interests including social norms, etc. https://www.dictionary.com/browse/nerd. Page 24

Neurodiversity – The notion that people, regardless of how different they appear, are located on the same neuro-spectrum, where no section is to be disrespected, since there is no "correct" way to think, or learn, or behave. Neurodiversity argues that neurological differences should not be view as deficiencies. https://www.health.harvard.edu/blog/what-is-neurodiversity-202111232645. Page 112

Neuroplasticity – The ability of the brain to create new connections, to adapt to new circumstances. https://facty.com/mind/how-neuroplasticity-affects-the-brain/. Page 75

O

OnX Backcountry and Offroad systems – Types of advanced global positioning systems that can be very helpful to the directionally challenged. https://buyersguide.org/off-road-GPS-unit/t/best? And https://www.scheels.com/p/onx-hunt-maps-chip-sd-card/15658-CA.html? Page 119

Orientation – A person's ability to be aware of his or her "self," in relation to our surroundings, at all times. https://neuronup.us/areas-of-intervention/cognitive-functions/. Page 130

Otoliths - Two small organs within the ear that detect movements of the head (moving up and down (heaving); left and right (swaying), or forward and backward). https://www.science-direct.com/topics/neuroscience/otolith. Page 72

P

Parallel park – "Unlike straight-in parking, the parallel version requires you to back into a space, turning just enough to fit in-between two other parked cars. As you move backwards and turn, you will need to avoid the car in front of you, the curb, anything near the curb (such as street signs), and the car behind you." https://www.tricountydrivingschool.org/parallel-parking-in-florida. Page 15

Phonics – A method for teaching reading and writing to beginners, usually young children. It's allowing the learner to hear and learn the sound of letters, and groups of letters that make up words. https://literacytrust.org.uk/information/what-is-literacy/what-phonics/. Page 10

Proprioceptive System – This is the system, made up of the neurological system, and the muscular skeletal system, that allows us to be aware of our limbs, where they are, and how to move them. https://www.continued.com/early-childhood-education/ask-the-experts/what-proprio-ceptive-system-and-does-23158? Page 72

Proprioception – This is your body's ability to sense movement, action, and location. It allows you to walk without consciously thinking where to place your foot next. It lets you touch your elbow, or the tip of your nose, with your eyes closed. Also known as kinesthesia. Page 74

R

Rasmussen's Encephalitis – A very rare form of encephalitis (inflammation of the brain), that gets progressively worse in one of the hemispheres to the point where no known treatment can help. Doctors are forced to contemplate removing the affected hemisphere. Also known as Rasmussen's syndrome. https://my.clevelandclinic.org/health/diseases/6092-rasmussens-encephalitis. Page 75

Reading Readiness – The point in the life of a young child when he or she starts recognizing that all the printed material they have been exposed to, contains words that can actually be pronounced, that make sense! https://www.splashlearn.com/blog/reading-readiness/. Page 53

Right-brain-dominant – The notion – not very established – that the right hemisphere of the brain is dominant. The dominance of the right hemisphere is allied with the dominance of the left side and the left hand. https://healthnile.com/quiz/left-brain-right-brain-test/?utm_source=google&utm_medium. Page 3

Right-hand dominant – Being able to do most activities, most notably, writing, with the right hand. https://www.webmd.com/brain/ss/slideshow-left-handed-vs-right. Page 89

Right hemisphere (of the Brain) – The right side of the brain. Page 32

Right-side-dominant – Being able to do most activities, most notably, writing, with the right hand, and being able to see better with the right eye, to hear better with the right ear, etc.

Road depth perception – Really, just depth perception, on the road. The ability to properly estimate the distance between the car being driven and vehicles ahead of and behind that vehicle. Your depth perception allows you to "see objects in three dimensions and understand how far away they are from you. Because your depth perception depends on information from both your eyes and your brain, anything affecting your overall vision can impact your depth perception." https://my.clevelandclinic.org/health/body/24956-depth-perception. Page 45

S

Semicircular Canals - Organs in the ear that also detect head movement. They "sense head rotations, arising either from self-induced movements or from angular accelerations of the head imparted by external forces." https://www.ncbi.nlm.nih.gov/books/NBK10863/.

Spatial dyslexia – Another term for directional challenge. https://www.reddit.com/r/adhdwomen/comments/1155glo/psa_spatial_dyslexia_is_a_lesser_known_learning/

Spatial navigation – The ability to know how to move from one point to another. https://www.ncbi.nlm.nih.gov/pmc/articles/PMC3380196/. Page 33

Spatial orientation – Our ability to handle information related to where we came from, where we are at any moment in time, where we're going, etc. https://neuronup.us/areas-of-intervention/cognitive-functions/. Page 73

T

Three-point turn – Turning around your vehicle on a narrow road, where a U-turn is impossible. https://www.driverlicense-school.com/florida-drivers-handbook/5-25.html. Page 15

Turned around – Seeing the surrounding from a different perspective from that seen before, even though nothing changed. Having the visual landscape flipped. https://blog. donders.ru.nl/?p=14135&lang=en. Page 80

V

Vestibular system – A complex set of structures and neural pathways that assist with our ability to locate ourselves and move to another point. https://www.ncbi.nlm.nih.gov/ books/NBK532978/ and https://www.ncbi.nlm.nih.gov/ books/NBK10819/. Page 72

Visual reorientation illusion (VRI) – The illusion that objects have shifted their position. Reportedly, this can be done voluntarily, but for most directionally challenged individuals, it can happen involuntarily. https://pubmed.ncbi.nlm.nih. gov/11430243/. Page 80

References

Bond, M. (2020). From here to there: The art of losing and finding our way. The Belknap Press of Harvard University Press. Cambridge, MA.

Casasanto, D. (2009). Embodiment of abstract concepts: Good and bad in right- and left-handers. Journal of Experimental Psychology: General, 138(3), 351–367. https://doi.org/10.1037/a0015854. Retrieved from: https://psycnet.apa.org/record/2009-11328-003

Casasanto, D. (2011). Different bodies, different minds: The body specificity of language and thought. Saga Journals. Volume 20. Issue 6. https://doi.org/10.1177/0963721411422058 retrieved from: https://journals.sagepub.com/doi/10.1177/0963721411422058

Cauffman, S., Cohen, M., et. Al. (2022). "I Am Here": Investigating the relationship between sense of direction and communication of spatial information. Proceedings of the Human Factors and Ergonomics Society Annual Meeting. Retrieved from: https://journals.sagepub.com/doi/abs/10.1177/1071181322661189

Condon, D., Wilt, J., Et. Al. (2015). Sense of direction: General factor saturation and associations with the Big-Five traits. Personality and Individual Differences, Volume 86, 2015, Pages 38-43, ISSN 0191-8869. Retrieved from: https://www.sciencedirect.com/science/article/abs/pii/S0191886915003578

Dahmani, L & Bohbot, V. Habitual use of GPS negatively impacts spatial memory during self-guided navigation. Retrieved from:

www.bic.mni.mcgill.ca/users/vero/PAPERS/Dahmani_
Bohbot_GPS_Scientific_Reports2020.pdf

Directional Dyslexia. Retrieved from https://www.dyslexia-reading-
well.com/

Gelling, C. (2021) Reading a Pacific navigator's mysterious map
may require a shift in perspective. Retrieved from: https://
knowablemagazine.org/content/article/society/2021/
reading-pacific-navigators-mysterious-map

Hegarty, M., Richardson, A. E., Montello, D. R., Lovelace, K., &
Subbiah, I. (2002). Development of a self-report measure of
environmental spatial ability. Intelligence, 30(5), 425-447. PDF

Holmes, B. (2024). Why do some people get lost? Retrieved
from: https://knowablemagazine.org/content/article/society/
2024/why-do-some-people-always-get-lost-but-others-dont

Hong, P. (2024). The science behind the left and right brain.
Retrieved from: https://scc.sa.utoronto.ca/content/
the-science-behind-the-left-and-right-brain/

Kemp, C. (2022). Dark and magical places: The neuroscience
of navigation. W. W. Norton & Company Inc. New York, NY.

Jabr, F. (2011). Cache Cab: Taxi drivers' brains grow to navigate
London's Streets. Scientific American. Retrieved from: https://
www.scientificamerican.com/article/london-taxi-memory/

Lefthandersday.com Retrieved from: the https://www.left-
handersday.com/tour9.html

Nguyen, K, Tansan, M., Newcombe, N. (2023). Studying the development of navigation using virtual environments. Retrieved
from: https://pubmed.ncbi.nlm.nih.gov/37614812/

www.ingramcontent.com/pod-product-compliance
Lightning Source LLC
Chambersburg PA
CBHW032054040426
42335CB00037B/707